GLORY TO THE FATHER

Glory to the Father,
    and to the Son,
    and to the Holy Spirit:
as it was in the beginning,
    is now,
    and will be for ever. Amen.

GLORIA AL PADRE

Gloria al Padre,
    y al Hijo,
    y al Espíritu Santo.
Como era en el principio,
    ahora y siempre,
    por los siglos de los siglos. Amén.

MORNING CANTICLE (Zechariah—*Benedictus*)
Luke 1:68-79

Blessed be the Lord God of Israel,
>   for he has looked favorably on his people and redeemed
>>   them.

He has raised up a mighty savior for us
>   in the house of his servant David,

as he spoke through the mouth of his holy prophets from
>   of old,
>>   that we would be saved from our enemies and from
>>> the hand of all who hate us.

Thus he has shown the mercy promised to our ancestors,
>   and has remembered his holy covenant,

the oath that he swore to our ancestor Abraham,
>   to grant us that we, being rescued from the hands of our
>>   enemies,

might serve him without fear, in holiness and righteousness
>   before him all our days.

And you, child, will be called the prophet of the Most High;
>   for you will go before the Lord to prepare his ways,

to give knowledge of salvation to his people
>   by the forgiveness of their sins.

By the tender mercy of our God,
>   the dawn from on high will break upon us,

to give light to those who sit in darkness and in the shadow of
>   death,
>>   to guide our feet into the way of peace.

EVENING CANTICLE (Mary—*Magnificat*)
  Luke 1:47-55

My soul magnifies the Lord,
  and my spirit rejoices in God my Savior,
for he has looked with favor on the lowliness of his servant.
  Surely, from now on all generations will call me blessed;
for the Mighty One has done great things for me,
  and holy is his name.
His mercy is for those who fear him
  from generation to generation.
He has shown strength with his arm;
  he has scattered the proud in the thoughts of their hearts.
He has brought down the powerful from their thrones,
  and lifted up the lowly;
he has filled the hungry with good things,
  and sent the rich away empty.
He has helped his servant Israel,
  in remembrance of his mercy,
according to the promise he made to our ancestors,
  to Abraham and to his descendants forever.

NIGHT CANTICLE (Simeon—*Nunc Dimittis*)
  Luke 2:29-32

Master, now you are dismissing your servant in peace,
  according to your word;
for my eyes have seen your salvation,
  which you have prepared in the presence of all peoples,
a light for revelation to the Gentiles
  and for glory to your people Israel.

THE LORD'S PRAYER

Our Father, who art in heaven,
hallowed be thy name;
thy kingdom come,
thy will be done
on earth as it is in heaven.
Give us this day our daily bread,
and forgive us our trespasses,
as we forgive those who trespass against us;
and lead us not into temptation,
but deliver us from evil. Amen.

PADRE NUESTRO

Padre nuestro, que estás en el cielo,
santificado sea tu nombre;
venga a nosotros tu reino;
hágase tu voluntad en la tierra como en el cielo.
Danos hoy nuestro pan de cada día;
perdona nuestras ofensas,
como también nosotros perdonamos
a los que nos ofenden;
no nos dejes caer en la tentación, y líbranos del mal.
Amén.

JUST PRAYER

JUST PRAYER

A BOOK OF HOURS FOR PEACEMAKERS AND JUSTICE SEEKERS

Alison M. Benders

LITURGICAL PRESS

Collegeville, Minnesota

www.litpress.org

1	2	3	4	5	6	7	8	9

Library of Congress Cataloging-in-Publication Data

Benders, Alison M.
    Just prayer : a book of hours for peacemakers and justice seekers / Alison M. Benders.
        pages   cm
    Includes bibliographical references.
    ISBN 978-0-8146-4966-4 — ISBN 978-0-8146-4991-6 (ebook)
    1. Prayer—Catholic Church—Study and teaching.   2. Prayers.
3. Christianity and justice—Catholic Church.   4. Bible—Quotations.
I. Title.

BV214.B47   2015
261.8—dc23   2014041394

To my parents, Pat and Ted Mearns,
who dedicated their lives to the service of justice,
and
To my husband, Larry, for standing by me.

CONTENTS

INTRODUCTION

Even though you offer me your burnt offerings and grain offerings,
*   I will not accept them . . .*
Take away from me the noise of your songs;
*   I will not listen to the melody of your harps.*
But let justice roll down like waters,
*   and righteousness like an ever-flowing stream.* (Amos 5:22-24)

Justice anchors our faith. It reaches back to the Torah and reso-
nates through the Christian Scriptures. Justice grounds Western
civilization. It provides the foundation for all communities and
societies across our planet. Justice expresses the deepest longing
of the human heart. Justice reveals the eternal nature of God.

The covenant between God and the Hebrew people marked
a fundamental shift in religious practice, known as the axial age.
The development marked a breathtaking moment for human
consciousness. In the Abrahamic traditions, believers shifted
from worshiping God to appease him to acting justly as a form
of worship. In the verses above from the prophet Amos, we hear
God rejecting piety and, in its stead, establishing justice as the
measure of faithfulness. God demands that people act as God
acts—with mercy, compassion, and love to create a world of
peaceful human flourishing.

We hear God's clear command to the Israelites: "Justice, and
only justice, you shall pursue" (Deut 16:20). Likewise, Jesus' ad-
monishment to his disciples recapitulates the whole of the Torah:
"Love God and love your neighbor as yourself." Love and justice

are inseparable because love, when it comes alive in our actions, *is* justice.

Justice

Often we hear the word "justice" and think of it as fairness. Fairness means following rules impartially, giving each person what is due. Yet justice is more than fairness. To understand justice, we have to move beyond autonomous individualism—away from the mentality of "what's in it for me?" This quid-pro-quo orientation is completely foreign to the Judeo-Christian meaning of justice. Justice is best understood as right relationship among people who live together.

In the Hebrew and Christian Scriptures, justice anchors human beings within their communities. Justice describes a communal life where each person flourishes, where each person is able to express his or her own human dignity. Justice has several dimensions when we actually practice it in our daily lives. *Commutative justice* seeks fairness as between individuals. People who are similarly situated should be treated similarly. *Distributive justice* allocates goods and burdens, rights and responsibilities, among community members. It recognizes that human beings are entitled to share in the bounty of creation. It also assures that those who reap benefits bear the costs, and those who build up society through their labor reap their share of the benefits. Finally, *contributive justice* concerns people's rights and duties to contribute to society. Contributive justice ensures that people can participate meaningfully to the structures and laws that govern their lives. Think here about the right to vote or the right to education, both of which are essential for self-determination. Thus, justice encompasses all the dimensions of human society. In our individually oriented culture, we can misunderstand justice to mean the protection of individual liberties. We need to begin thinking in terms of systems and institutions. Justice focuses on how we treat people, how we share benefits and responsibilities, and how we assure that everyone sits at the table.

Justice, then, is about community life. Individuals and the community are complementary. Our human community is an economic reality, certainly. Yet it is even more a spiritual, psychological, political, and physical reality. Every day we depend on other human beings to live. We do nothing and have nothing in isolation from those who grow our food, make our clothes, share our cities, and breathe the air with us. Not just in theory—but really and truly—we are one human family bound together in creation with a shared destiny. In seeking justice, we must remember that just relationships promote the well-being of the individual person within the community. It is true that "all boats rise together." The moral challenge to each of us is to create a new identity where we know ourselves as bound to others in relationship with them, rather than in competition against them. When our good is linked with that of other people and with the whole community, we will choose more just solutions for the common good.

So how can we tell if our actions are truly leading toward justice? How can we tell if we are having an impact? Measuring justice in a community means examining the lives of the poorest and most marginalized from their perspective. Clearly, we understand the unjust conditions that permeate our communities when we have experienced them, either as victims or in service to those who suffer directly. Direct experience gives us a powerful understanding of painful suffering. We can also listen to people who entreat us for justice. We can look with them into their lives to understand whether justice is retreating or advancing. What are the prospects for women, for immigrants, for those who have no money or no power? Are opportunities for education, jobs, and health care really organized to support better lives for people, or do these services alleviate suffering only temporarily? In the final accounting, the lives of all people taken together are the measure of justice, especially the *anawim*, the least among us.

Prayer

In our troubled times, the sight of suffering moves our hearts. And so it should. We owe compassion to refugees, the impoverished, orphans, and all who suffer exclusion and oppression. More than that, we owe our fellow human beings just communities and peaceful places to live. Yet changing our habits and beliefs requires more than a sympathetic feeling. Change means more than charity and occasional service. Two strands of practice must intersect in us to establish justice for permanent change. First and obviously, we have to create relationships, institutions, and communities ruled by just practices. Second, and perhaps equally obvious, we need to change ourselves.

For meaningful personal change, we have to link our experiences of human suffering with God's revealed justice. Prayer—moved by God's own Spirit of Peace—is the link. *Just Prayer* seeks to offer a path to connect action and transformation through devotions focused on justice—just prayer. Prayer is more than petition. Prayer is relationship with God. Praying draws us into the love of God. It sustains our work and our growth to become more like God in our thoughts and actions. Through reflection, repetition, practice, and, of course, grace, we conform our minds and hearts to the justice that expresses God's promise of peace.

We also pray because prayer brings us into God's heart just as it did for Jesus. From the moment of Jesus' conception, with Mary's prayerful yes to God's will, to his last words commending his spirit to the Father, Jesus prayed. Jesus retreated in quiet prayer every morning to draw strength from God for the day's work ahead. He prayed the ancient blessing at meals, recognizing that our lives are a gift: "Blessed are you, God of all creation." Jesus prayed over the few fishes and the small loaves before he fed the thousands who listened to his teaching. He prayed before calling Lazarus out of the tomb. With the Lord's Prayer, Jesus taught his disciples to pray to God daily for all their needs. Most importantly, he instructed them, "Pray always." Thus, we pray because Jesus told us to do so, confident that prayer transforms us.

Just Prayer conforms to the most traditional rhythms of Judeo-Christian worship. It is carefully patterned on the Christian community's ageless Liturgy of the Hours, also known as the Divine Office. The Christian practices, in their turn, draw upon the ancient practice among Jews to pray the psalms. The individual Offices, from dawn through night, are consecrated with psalms, canticles, and readings from Scriptures. Customarily, the Divine Office will include Scripture passages and petitions relevant to the liturgical year. Communities of monks generally recited the Offices together, but the Hours can also be prayed silently or aloud as an individual spiritual practice.

In this revered tradition, *Just Prayer* presents a four-week cycle of morning and evening prayer reflecting on themes of justice, or its absence. The morning and evening Offices select compelling Scripture passages that call us into the life of God. Individual days focus on pressing problems around the globe, such as poverty, violence, or environmental degradation. The Offices present Scripture readings, reflections, and prayers that complement active service in the world. While the intercessions offer traditional petitions for God's direct blessing on those in need, they more often focus our attention on personal transformation and systemic change. Whatever our level of service, these morning and evening devotions draw our experiences and emotions together into prayerful reflection. By complementing our works of service in the community, *Just Prayer* can help us conform our hearts and our lives to the Christian vision of justice. Over a series of days or weeks, the cycle of carefully selected texts allows us to experience, understand, desire, practice, and celebrate justice. As the Divine Office has always done, *Just Prayer* can help us to respond more fully to the vision of a just community that God has set before us.

Just Prayer

Just Prayer expresses four biblical themes related to justice and injustice, as we experience them in our lives. The cycle weaves together feelings and images that lead us from resisting justice to celebrating its promised triumph.

1. *Justice Ordained*: The first week's readings and prayers proclaim that God has established justice as the fundamental relationship among people. The readings also recognize that people resist living justly; they call out the suffering this can cause.

2. *Injustice Lamented*: The second week's prayers invite us to grieve with the misery of others. The readings allow us to lament with suffering victims, acknowledging their weariness and hopelessness. Lamentation echoes the weeping of the people of Israel in exile from their land. It voices the plight of marginalized people around the globe.

3. *Justice Practiced*: The third week's focus on practicing justice begins the journey toward reducing and eliminating injustice. Its images focus on forgiveness, reconciliation, and transformation. This week encourages us to recognize how we have failed to live in community and how we might build more just relationships among people in our world.

4. *Justice Celebrated*: The theme for the fourth and final week celebrates justice. In our current society, justice is more aspirational than achieved; it is a hope, not yet a fact. Still, the readings thrill with the image of a new community, the reign of God, where God's promised justice will be the heart of our human lives together.

The four weeks of morning and evening Offices promote intentional change. In praying through these themes, we move from knowing God's command to live justly, through sharing the misery of injustice to reconciliation and a renewed commitment to justice, to celebrating finally God's promise of a new order. Through emotional engagement, complemented by daily reflection on our experiences and current events, we can become more deeply and personally committed to justice. The Offices in *Just Prayer* presuppose that people praying this cycle are actively engaged in service or ministry, although anyone living attentively in the world cannot fail to see the injustices around us. Both practical experience and thoughtful reflection give human faces to the consequences of our sin. However, the cycle does not end with shame or what we have failed to do. Rather, the final weeks bring us through recommitment and renewal to joy and thanksgiving. We are grateful for God's grace, which redeems us through Christ. In the hope and promise of justice, we pray together for our human communities now and for the generations to come.

Using *Just Prayer*

Very practically, using *Just Prayer* means two things. We can think first about the quality of the prayer. The power of the Liturgy of the Hours lies in the ancient rhythms of give and take, call and response, and above all in repetition. Like a song whose notes must ring according to the measure and beat of the lyrics, the words of the psalms flow in poetic meter. The pacing during the Office should be reflective and measured. Groups praying the Offices out loud should resist the urge to rush to the end. Instead, the morning and evening prayer should be allowed to seep slowly into our hearts and shape our lives. The repeated verses and rituals give us words and images to shape our lives even after the cycle is finished. People praying these Offices may choose to stick with the basic cycle because repetition often brings deeper insight and lasting impact, or may choose their own readings to highlight particular perspectives.

More specifically, there are four seven-day cycles of morning and evening Offices, one cycle in each chapter. Each chapter begins and ends with a brief reflection on the weekly theme. These essays explain the theme, underline a few of the key ideas in the readings, and provide questions for deeper reflection. Customarily, the Office is prayed with the assistance of a leader and two alternating groups or choirs. Much of the advice below presumes a group setting. However, the Offices can always be prayed alone, with our hearts joined to people around the globe who are also praying the Divine Office.

- *Opening greeting*: The leader calls the group to attention and opens the prayer. To begin the Office, groups might develop their own opening gesture, such as signing the cross, ringing a bell, or sitting still for several calming breaths.

- *Invitatory couplets*: All the Offices begin by inviting the presence of the Spirit. Here, each starts with the couplet, "Lord, teach us justice. / And we shall live in your peace." At the start of the Office, the couplet opens our hearts to God's grace and offers our work for the good of all. The justice/peace couplet replaces the traditional morning verse, "Lord, open my lips. / And my mouth will proclaim your praise," and evening verse, "God, come to my assistance. Lord, make haste to help me." These verses might be substituted to remain faithful to the traditional Office. Repeating the couplet morning, evening, and throughout the day as an act of prayer refocuses our hearts and actions.

- *Psalm*: The morning and evening devotions open with a single psalm voicing the emotions and concerns of the weekly theme. At the beginning of the psalm, the response (designated by ℟) summarizes the intention for the week; the verse remains the same for the whole week. The psalm should be recited together by groups and even out loud when we are alone. Large groups can be split into two choirs to alternate reading aloud. They can recite the psalm response after each psalm paragraph or wait until the end, using the response to summarize the meaning of the psalm. After the last verse of the psalm, the group recites the doxology (prayer of praise), "Glory to the Father." The text of this prayer is set forth in both English and Spanish at the front and back of this book.

- *Reading*: One person can be appointed to read the Scripture passage, from the Hebrew Scriptures in the morning and the Gospels in the evening. The readings highlight Judeo-Christian teachings on justice and show how justice can be practiced. The readings can be customized by substituting alternative Scripture passages from Christianity or any other religious tradition. Groups might also consider essays, reflections, homilies, or poems that suit their work, concerns, or culture.

- *Silent reflection*: The evening prayer cycle establishes a moment of silent reflection after the gospel. While the traditional format for the Liturgy of the Hours does not include a homily or sermon, depending upon the size and purpose of the gathering, someone might offer a brief reflection on the readings of the day.

- *Optional canticles*: The traditional morning Office includes the Canticle of Zechariah and the evening Office has the Canticle of Mary, also known as the *Magnificat*. These have been omitted from the daily Offices in *Just Prayer*, but the texts of these canticles are reprinted at the front and back of this book for people who desire to pray them regularly. These canticles are usually prayed after the Scripture passages and before the intercessions. The Canticle of Simeon, customarily recited as part of the night Office just before retiring, is also included to complete the cycle of the Hours, as an optional private devotion.

- *Intercessions*: Intercessions follow immediately after the readings in the morning and after the reflection in the evening. Groups may pray the suggested petitions or personalize them according to their experiences during the day. The petitions allow a moment to add individual names and needs offered to God's special care. After each individual petition, the group responds with the verses provided or with "Lord, hear our prayer."

- *The Lord's Prayer*: The Lord's Prayer (Our Father) signals the closing sequence as participants place themselves in the presence of God and acknowledge God's will. The text of the Lord's Prayer in English and Spanish is printed at the front and back of this prayer book.

- *Sharing of Peace*: All of the devotions end with the sharing of peace. Like many elements of the Liturgy of the Hours and the Christian Mass, the sharing of peace finds its roots in the Hebrew greeting "shalom." The leader might initiate the sharing of peace with an invitation such as, "Let us offer a gesture of peace, of God's shalom, to one another." Groups ought to share the peace of God with each other according to their own community customs. When we pray the Offices alone, we can offer peace to others from the silence of our hearts.

- *Closing Prayer*: After sharing peace, the leader or another participant will offer the closing prayer, or final blessing, to send people to work or to their nightly rest. The closing prayers in each section collect the ideas from the week and the daily theme into a petition for special attention.

According to the Christian custom, every weekly cycle begins with Sunday morning. The full cycle imitates the rhythms of a workweek and the moods of morning and evening as it builds toward fuller meaning with the approach of Saturday evening. Thus, whether groups are on retreat for only a weekend or for a week or more, the prayer cycle moves emotionally and prayerfully to culminate in the weekend Offices. Friday remains a day of repentance in every thematic cycle, honoring Christ's death on Good Friday. There are many choices to customize the Offices:

One week retreat:
- Select the most relevant theme and pray the days as scheduled.
- Pray Sunday morning and evening for weeks 1, 2, and 3, then pray morning and evening on Thursday, Friday, Saturday, and Sunday for week 4.

One long weekend retreat:
- Use morning and evening Offices from the Sunday of each of the four weeks.

One day retreat:
- Select the most relevant theme and then use Friday, Saturday, or Sunday prayer.

Lent:
- Ash Wednesday through the fourth week of Lent, use weeks 1–4 of *Just Prayer.*
- Fifth week of Lent, use either week 1 (*Justice Ordained*) or week 2 (*Injustice Lamented*).
- Holy Week
  - Monday through Good Friday, use the corresponding days of week 3 (*Justice Practiced*).
  - Holy Saturday and Easter Sunday, use the corresponding days of week 4 (*Justice Celebrated*).

Thematically—to focus on a particular area of need, select a day from each week, as follows:
- Sundays—poverty and want of any sort
- Mondays—war and violence

- Tuesdays—immigration and refugees
- Wednesdays—environment and climate health
- Thursdays—human health and well-being
- Fridays—justice for women and children
- Saturdays—inequality between social, economic, racial, religious, ethnic, and gender classes

Any Office can be customized with additional readings on social issues, with hymns or music, and with litanies that the participants write. The bibliography offers resources for prayers and additional reading on social justice. Repetition and variety both have their places in prayer. What matters most is persistence if we are to open ourselves fully to God's grace.

Hope for Justice and Peace

Isaiah's words still call us today: "They shall beat their swords into plowshares, / and their spears into pruning hooks; / nation shall not lift up sword against nation, / neither shall they learn war any more" (2:4). Certainly we must strive for justice, whether that is in our home communities or in areas of desolation and strife. We must beat our swords into plowshares, our spears into pruning hooks. So, above all, we—we ourselves—must practice the ways of justice and peace. Yet the great struggle is the internal one . . . the struggle to become perfect justice as our God is perfect justice. *Just Prayer* will support the transforming work of justice and peace.

JUSTICE ORDAINED

RECOGNIZING GOD'S COMMAND TO LIVE JUSTLY

All human societies have longed for justice as the foundation of a peaceful life. Justice means that people are fed and secure in their homes. It means that they are free to seek a good life, and are able to love and long for God. God ordains justice. As Isaiah declares, "Is [the Lord's command] not to share your bread with the hungry, / and bring the homeless poor into your house; / when you see the naked, to cover them, / and not to hide yourself from your own kin?" (58:7). God commands us to be just as the most authentic way to live together. This command is not foreign or strange. We find justice commanded both in Scripture and in our hearts as our deepest longing. Just action expresses the very nature of God that we share as God's children.

God's just command is as old as civilization, yet we must hear it over and over again until we become transformed into just people. The readings for this week help us cultivate justice in our hearts and actions. Overall, they highlight God's command to live justly, which is drawn from the psalms and other Hebrew texts. We hear the voices of the great prophets Isaiah and Jeremiah, who call the people to amend their ways and live righteously. We hear how sweet God's law is; the covenant celebrated in the book of Deuteronomy expresses both God's nature and our desire for a world that makes sense. The readings also give us examples

1

of justice in the Christian gospels. We hear Jesus' Sermon on the Mount, using the kingdom of God as the image for the just human community. We also listen to his followers debate the question of justice with him. Many of the readings link just action with God's favor and reward. This reward is not for ourselves only, but is shared with our neighbors and community because justice yields peace.

The psalm response for this week, "People who practice justice, walk in the light of God," hearkens back to Isaiah and the great prophets. It reminds us that God ordains justice, while also intimating that the consequence of justice is peace. Repeated daily, the verse provides us with a ready adage to focus our thoughts and prayers on God's fundamental command. It also recapitulates the witness of Christ's life, as the one who lived God's justice perfectly. The intercessions invite us to recognize that justice is both God's command and the path to a flourishing community. As we pray throughout the week, we can reflect on how we hear and respond to God's command to live with justice.

SUNDAY MORNING

✝

Lord, teach us justice.
And we shall live in your peace.

PSALM 50:1-2, 4-8, 14-15
℟ People who practice justice, walk in the light of God.

The mighty one, God the LORD,
   speaks and summons the earth
   from the rising of the sun to its setting.
Out of Zion, the perfection of beauty,
   God shines forth. . . .

He calls to the heavens above
   and to the earth, that he may judge his people:
"Gather to me my faithful ones,
   who made a covenant with me by sacrifice!"
The heavens declare his righteousness,
   for God himself is judge.

"Hear, O my people, and I will speak,
   O Israel, I will testify against you.
   I am God, your God.
Not for your sacrifices do I rebuke you;
   your burnt offerings are continually before me. . . .

"Offer to God a sacrifice of thanksgiving,
    and pay your vows to the Most High.
Call on me in the day of trouble;
    I will deliver you, and you shall glorify me."

Glory to the Father . . .

SCRIPTURE   Isaiah 58:7-10
Is [the Lord's command] not to share your bread with the hungry,
    and bring the homeless poor into your house;
when you see the naked, to cover them,
    and not to hide yourself from your own kin?
Then your light shall break forth like the dawn,
    and your healing shall spring up quickly;
your vindicator shall go before you,
    the glory of the LORD shall be your rear guard.
Then you shall call, and the LORD will answer;
    you shall cry for help, and he will say, Here I am.
If you remove the yoke from among you,
    the pointing of the finger, the speaking of evil,
if you offer your food to the hungry
    and satisfy the needs of the afflicted,
then your light shall rise in the darkness
    and your gloom be like the noonday.

The Word of the Lord.

INTERCESSIONS
Spirit of Hope, your creation offers sustenance to satisfy all our
needs and you command us to care for all people as our neighbors. Yet so many people in the world live in poverty. So we pray

today for people who suffer from scarcity and need: *Lord, open our hearts to the poor among us.*

- Rouse us to feed the hungry, shelter the homeless, and protect those sickened through deprivation. We pray to the Lord.
- Bless those who work for the elimination of economic injustice and let their work prosper. We pray to the Lord.
- Transform our hearts today to become more compassionate and generous to children, women, and men who are living in need. We pray to the Lord.
- For what else shall we pray this morning? [Pause for participants to add their own intentions.] We pray to the Lord.

THE LORD'S PRAYER
With these petitions in our hearts, we pray as the Lord taught us:
Our Father . . .

SHARING OF PEACE

CLOSING PRAYER
May the God of Abundance bless the work of our hands today. May God bring justice and plenty into the lives of people near and far. We ask this in Christ's name. AMEN.

SUNDAY EVENING

✝

Lord, teach us justice.
And we shall live in your peace.

PSALM 81:8-14, 16
℟ People who practice justice, walk in the light of God.

"Hear, O my people, while I admonish you;
    O Israel, if you would but listen to me!
There shall be no strange god among you;
    you shall not bow down to a foreign god.

I am the LORD your God,
    who brought you up out of the land of Egypt.
    Open your mouth wide and I will fill it.

"But my people did not listen to my voice;
    Israel would not submit to me.
So I gave them over to their stubborn hearts,
    to follow their own counsels.
O that my people would listen to me,
    that Israel would walk in my ways!
Then I would quickly subdue their enemies,
    and turn my hand against their foes. . . .

I would feed you with the finest of the wheat,
    and with honey from the rock I would satisfy you."

Glory to the Father . . .

SCRIPTURE   Matthew 5:1-12

When Jesus saw the crowds, he went up the mountain; and after
  he sat down, his disciples came to him. Then he began to
  speak, and taught them, saying:

'Blessed are the poor in spirit, for theirs is the kingdom of heaven.

'Blessed are those who mourn, for they will be comforted.

'Blessed are the meek, for they will inherit the earth.

'Blessed are those who hunger and thirst for righteousness,
  for they will be filled.

'Blessed are the merciful, for they will receive mercy.

'Blessed are the pure in heart, for they will see God.

'Blessed are the peacemakers, for they will be called children
  of God.

'Blessed are those who are persecuted for righteousness' sake,
  for theirs is the kingdom of heaven.

'Blessed are you when people revile you and persecute you and
  utter all kinds of evil against you falsely on my account. Rejoice and be glad, for your reward is great in heaven, for in the
  same way they persecuted the prophets who were before you.

The Gospel of the Lord.

SILENT REFLECTION

INTERCESSIONS

Spirit of Hope, we witness the tragedy poverty visits upon your
people. Pour your compassion into our hearts so we will use our
plenty to eliminate poverty and its miseries from the lives of
others. And so we pray: *Lord, open our hearts to the poor among
us.*

- Move us to share your abundant blessings more justly among all nations and all people. We pray to the Lord.
- Inspire leaders in every community to recognize the plight of the poor and respond with solutions that are just, dignified, and permanent. We pray to the Lord.
- For people whose lives are narrowed by the struggle for daily needs, especially for [pause for participants to add individual names or needs]. We pray to the Lord.
- For what else shall we pray because of our experiences today? [Pause for participants to add their own intentions.] We pray to the Lord.

THE LORD'S PRAYER
With these petitions in our hearts, we pray as the Lord taught us:
Our Father . . .

SHARING OF PEACE

CLOSING PRAYER
May the God of Abundance grant us the wisdom of Christ to practice justice and the grace of the Holy Spirit to persist until we succeed. AMEN.

MONDAY MORNING

✝

Lord, teach us justice.
And we shall live in your peace.

PSALM 37:1-6, 8, 18-19, 23-24
℟ People who practice justice, walk in the light of God.

Do not fret because of the wicked;
    do not be envious of wrongdoers,
for they will soon fade like the grass,
    and wither like the green herb.

Trust in the LORD, and do good;
    so you will live in the land, and enjoy security.
Take delight in the LORD,
    and he will give you the desires of your heart.

Commit your way to the LORD;
    trust in him, and he will act.
He will make your vindication shine like the light,
    and the justice of your cause like the noonday. . . .
Refrain from anger, and forsake wrath.
    Do not fret—it leads only to evil. . . .

The LORD knows the days of the blameless,
    and their heritage will abide forever;

they are not put to shame in evil times,
    in the days of famine they have abundance. . . .

Our steps are made firm by the Lord,
    when he delights in our way;
though we stumble, we shall not fall headlong,
    for the Lord holds us by the hand.

Glory to the Father . . .

SCRIPTURE   Sirach 15:14-20

It was [the Lord] who created humankind in the beginning,
    and he left them in the power of their own free choice.
If you choose, you can keep the commandments,
    and to act faithfully is a matter of your own choice.
He has placed before you fire and water;
    stretch out your hand for whichever you choose.
Before each person are life and death,
    and whichever one chooses will be given.
For great is the wisdom of the Lord;
    he is mighty in power and sees everything;
his eyes are on those who fear him,
    and he knows every human action.
He has not commanded anyone to be wicked,
    and he has not given anyone permission to sin.

The Word of the Lord.

INTERCESSIONS

God of Mercy, your son Jesus Christ taught us the way of peace and compassion, which you ordained from the foundation of the world. Still, the daily conflicts and the unending wars in our world expose our failure to follow his example. And so we pray today for peace in our hearts and in our world: *Lord, may peace reign in our hearts and in our lives.*

- Heal the bodies and spirits of victims of war, aggression, and violence of any kind. We pray to the Lord.
- Bless and multiply the efforts of peacekeepers, mediators, intercessors, and healers to end violence and restore security. We pray to the Lord.
- Teach all people of goodwill to resolve their differences peacefully. We pray to the Lord.
- For what else shall we pray this morning? [Pause for participants to add their own intentions.] We pray to the Lord.

THE LORD'S PRAYER

With these petitions in our hearts, we pray as the Lord taught us: Our Father . . .

SHARING OF PEACE

CLOSING PRAYER

May the God of Peace bless the work of our hands today and through our actions bring greater tranquility and security into the world. We ask this in Christ's name. AMEN.

MONDAY EVENING

✝

Lord, teach us justice.
And we shall live in your peace.

PSALM 26:1-8
℞ People who practice justice, walk in the light of God.

Vindicate me, O LORD,
    for I have walked in my integrity,
    and I have trusted in the LORD without wavering.
Prove me, O LORD, and try me;
    test my heart and mind.
For your steadfast love is before my eyes,
    and I walk in faithfulness to you.

I do not sit with the worthless,
    nor do I consort with hypocrites;
I hate the company of evildoers,
    and will not sit with the wicked.

I wash my hands in innocence,
    and go around your altar, O LORD,
singing aloud a song of thanksgiving,
    and telling all your wondrous deeds.

O LORD, I love the house in which you dwell,
    and the place where your glory abides.

Glory to the Father . . .

SCRIPTURE   Mark 12:28-34

One of the scribes came near and heard them disputing with one another, and seeing that [Jesus] answered them well, he asked him, "Which commandment is the first of all?" Jesus answered, "The first is, 'Hear, O Israel: the Lord our God, the Lord is one; you shall love the Lord your God with all your heart, and with all your soul, and with all your mind, and with all your strength.' The second is this: 'You shall love your neighbor as yourself.' There is no other commandment greater than these." Then the scribe said to him, "You are right, Teacher; you have truly said that 'he is one, and besides him there is no other'; and 'to love him with all the heart, and with all the understanding, and with all the strength,' and 'to love one's neighbor as oneself,'—this is much more important than all whole burnt offerings and sacrifices." When Jesus saw that he had answered wisely, he said to him, "You are not far from the kingdom of God." After that no one dared to ask him any question.

The Gospel of the Lord.

SILENT REFLECTION

INTERCESSIONS

Spirit of Mercy, we have witnessed how violence of all kinds diminishes and distorts human lives. Only gentleness, humility, and mercy will repair our stricken world. And so we pray: *Lord, may peace reign in our hearts and in our lives.*

- Console families who have lost children, parents, friends, and loved ones to violence. We pray to the Lord.

- Grant us the courage to examine our lives and repair the violence we have inflicted on others. We pray to the Lord.
- Restore security to all communities in our world that are not safe and protect the lives of the residents, especially [pause for participants to add individual names or needs]. We pray to the Lord.
- For what else shall we pray because of our experiences today? [Pause for participants to add their own intentions.] We pray to the Lord.

THE LORD'S PRAYER
With these petitions in our hearts, we pray as the Lord taught us:
Our Father . . .

SHARING OF PEACE

CLOSING PRAYER
May the God of Peace enable us to stand by those who suffer violence and to work for a new order based on justice and goodwill. We ask in Christ's name. AMEN.

TUESDAY MORNING

✝

Lord, teach us justice.
And we shall live in your peace.

PSALM 112:1-9
R℣ People who practice justice, walk in the light of God.

Praise the LORD!
   Happy are those who fear the LORD,
      who greatly delight in his commandments.
Their descendants will be mighty in the land;
      the generation of the upright will be blessed.
Wealth and riches are in their houses,
      and their righteousness endures forever.
They rise in the darkness as a light for the upright;
      they are gracious, merciful, and righteous.
It is well with those who deal generously and lend,
      who conduct their affairs with justice.
For the righteous will never be moved;
      they will be remembered forever.
They are not afraid of evil tidings;
      their hearts are firm, secure in the LORD.
Their hearts are steady, they will not be afraid . . .

They have distributed freely, they have given to the poor;
  their righteousness endures forever;
  their horn is exalted in honor.

Glory to the Father . . .

SCRIPTURE   Deuteronomy 24:14-15, 17, 19
You shall not withhold the wages of poor and needy laborers,
whether other Israelites or aliens who reside in your land in one
of your towns. You shall pay them their wages daily before sunset,
because they are poor and their livelihood depends on them;
otherwise they might cry to the LORD against you, and you would
incur guilt. . . .

You shall not deprive a resident alien or an orphan of justice; you
shall not take a widow's garment in pledge. . . .

When you reap your harvest in your field and forget a sheaf in the
field, you shall not go back to get it; it shall be left for the alien,
the orphan, and the widow, so that the LORD your God may bless
you in all your undertakings.

The Word of the Lord.

INTERCESSIONS
God for Others, your prophets throughout the ages have exhorted
us to welcome strangers and travelers into our communities.
Immigrants and refugees need welcome more than ever in our
global society. So we pray today for the unity of all humanity:
Lord, teach us to welcome each person who comes to us in need.

- Bless immigrants and refugees with welcoming and safe neighbors. We pray to the Lord.

- Assist people fleeing violence in their communities to find the resources they need to restore and rebuild their lives. We pray to the Lord.

- Inspire communities of safety and plenty to share their resources generously with people seeking asylum. We pray to the Lord.

- For what else shall we pray this morning? [Pause for participants to add their own intentions.] We pray to the Lord.

THE LORD'S PRAYER

With these petitions in our hearts, we pray as the Lord taught us: Our Father . . .

SHARING OF PEACE

CLOSING PRAYER

May the God of Welcome bless the work of our hands today and, through our actions, create communities of goodness and hospitality. We ask this in Christ's name. AMEN.

TUESDAY EVENING

✝

Lord, teach us justice.
And we shall live in your peace.

PSALM 15
R̸ People who practice justice, walk in the light of God.

O LORD, who may abide in your tent?
      Who may dwell on your holy hill?

Those who walk blamelessly, and do what is right,
      and speak the truth from their heart;
who do not slander with their tongue,
      and do no evil to their friends,
      nor take up a reproach against their neighbors;
in whose eyes the wicked are despised,
      but who honor those who fear the LORD;
who stand by their oath even to their hurt;
who do not lend money at interest,
      and do not take a bribe against the innocent.

Those who do these things shall never be moved.

Glory to the Father . . .

SCRIPTURE   Luke 11:33-36
[Jesus spoke to them:] "No one after lighting a lamp puts it in a
cellar, but on the lampstand so that those who enter may see the
light. Your eye is the lamp of your body. If your eye is healthy,

your whole body is full of light; but if it is not healthy, your body is full of darkness. Therefore consider whether the light in you is not darkness. If then your whole body is full of light, with no part of it in darkness, it will be as full of light as when a lamp gives you light with its rays."

The Gospel of the Lord.

SILENT REFLECTION

INTERCESSIONS

Holy Spirit, we know the heartache of people displaced because of human and natural disasters. Show us how we can offer light and hope to ease their misery. And so we pray: *Lord, teach us to welcome each person who comes to us in need.*

- Give us courage to examine our assumptions about strangers and teach us to recognize them as sisters and brothers of goodwill. We pray to the Lord.

- Rouse leaders of every nation to protect migrant workers and secure for them just wages and fair treatment. We pray to the Lord.

- Reunite immigrants and travelers with their children, parents, friends, and loved ones who have been left behind, especially [pause for participants to add individual names or needs]. We pray to the Lord.

- For what else shall we pray because of our experiences today? [Pause for participants to add their own intentions.] We pray to the Lord.

THE LORD'S PRAYER
With these petitions in our hearts, we pray as the Lord taught us:
Our Father . . .

SHARING OF PEACE

CLOSING PRAYER
May the God of Welcome fill our hearts with the hospitality, warmth, and tenderness that is necessary to sustain one human family worldwide. We ask in Christ's name. AMEN.

WEDNESDAY MORNING

✝

Lord, teach us justice.
And we shall live in your peace.

PSALM 19:7-11, 14
℟ People who practice justice, walk in the light of God.

The law of the LORD is perfect,
    reviving the soul;
the decrees of the LORD are sure,
    making wise the simple;
the precepts of the LORD are right,
    rejoicing the heart;
the commandment of the LORD is clear,
    enlightening the eyes;
the fear of the LORD is pure,
    enduring forever;
the ordinances of the LORD are true
    and righteous altogether.
More to be desired are they than gold,
    even much fine gold;
sweeter also than honey,
    and drippings of the honeycomb.

Moreover by them is your servant warned;
    in keeping them there is great reward. . . .

Let the words of my mouth and the meditation of my heart
   be acceptable to you,
   O LORD, my rock and my redeemer.

Glory to the Father . . .

SCRIPTURE   Jeremiah 7:2-7
Hear the word of the LORD, all you people of Judah, you that enter
these gates to worship the LORD. Thus says the LORD of hosts,
the God of Israel: Amend your ways and your doings, and let
me dwell with you in this place. Do not trust in these deceptive
words: "This is the temple of the LORD, the temple of the LORD,
the temple of the LORD."

For if you truly amend your ways and your doings, if you truly
act justly one with another, if you do not oppress the alien, the
orphan, and the widow, or shed innocent blood in this place, and
if you do not go after other gods to your own hurt, then I will
dwell with you in this place, in the land that I gave of old to your
ancestors forever and ever.

The Word of the Lord.

INTERCESSIONS
God of Creation, you have blessed our earth with life and com-
mended it to our care. So we pray today for the wisdom to safeguard the earth for all creatures who call it home: *Wellspring of
Life, make us just stewards of the earth and its blessings.*

- Teach us to appreciate the natural world and give us wisdom to protect our planet for future generations. We pray to the Lord.

- Rouse us to urgent action to protect the earth from the impact of our economic activities. We pray to the Lord.

- Make us always grateful for the sun in the day and the moon and stars at night. We pray to the Lord.

- For what else shall we pray this morning? [Pause for participants to add their own intentions.] We pray to the Lord.

THE LORD'S PRAYER
With these petitions in our hearts, we pray as the Lord taught us:
Our Father . . .

SHARING OF PEACE

CLOSING PRAYER
May the God of Day and Night dwell with us today and, through our actions, bring forth the earth's bounty for all to share. We ask this in Christ's name. AMEN.

WEDNESDAY EVENING

✟

Lord, teach us justice.
And we shall live in your peace.

PSALM 1
R⁊ People who practice justice, walk in the light of God.

Happy are those
   who do not follow the advice of the wicked,
or take the path that sinners tread,
   or sit in the seat of scoffers;
but their delight is in the law of the LORD,
   and on his law they meditate day and night.
They are like trees
   planted by streams of water,
which yield their fruit in its season,
   and their leaves do not wither.
In all that they do, they prosper.
The wicked are not so,
   but are like chaff that the wind drives away.
Therefore the wicked will not stand in the judgment,
   nor sinners in the congregation of the righteous;
for the LORD watches over the way of the righteous,
   but the way of the wicked will perish.

Glory to the Father . . .

SCRIPTURE   Mark 9:33-37

[Jesus and his disciples] came to Capernaum; and when he was in the house he asked them, "What were you arguing about on the way?" But they were silent, for on the way they had argued with one another who was the greatest. He sat down, called the twelve, and said to them, "Whoever wants to be first must be last of all and servant of all." Then [Jesus] took a little child and put it among them; and taking it in his arms, he said to them, "Whoever welcomes one such child in my name welcomes me, and whoever welcomes me welcomes not me but the one who sent me."

The Gospel of the Lord.

SILENT REFLECTION

INTERCESSIONS

Spirit of Creation, you fashioned our world and showered it with beauty beyond telling. Every woman, man, and child depends upon the health and bounty of this planet we call our home. And so we pray: *Wellspring of Life, make us just stewards of the earth and its blessings.*

- Make us grateful for pure water, clean air, and safe soils that give us life. We pray to the Lord.
- Teach us to protect all plants and animals that live on earth and to recognize our human responsibilities as caretakers of creation. We pray to the Lord.
- Safeguard the poor who disproportionately suffer from natural disasters and human pollution, especially [pause for participants to add individual names or needs]. We pray to the Lord.

- For what else shall we pray because of our experiences today? [Pause for participants to add their own intentions.] We pray to the Lord.

THE LORD'S PRAYER

With these petitions in our hearts, we pray as the Lord taught us: Our Father . . .

SHARING OF PEACE

CLOSING PRAYER

May the God of Day and Night heal our world, bestow abundance on our lands, and plant justice in our hearts. We ask in Christ's name. AMEN.

THURSDAY MORNING

✝

Lord, teach us justice.
And we shall live in your peace.

PSALM 78:1-7
℟ People who practice justice, walk in the light of God.

Give ear, O my people, to my teaching;
    incline your ears to the words of my mouth.
I will open my mouth in a parable;
    I will utter dark sayings from of old,
things that we have heard and known,
    that our ancestors have told us.
We will not hide them from their children;
    we will tell to the coming generation
the glorious deeds of the LORD, and his might,
    and the wonders that he has done.

He established a decree in Jacob,
    and appointed a law in Israel,
which he commanded our ancestors
    to teach to their children;
that the next generation might know them,
    the children yet unborn,

and rise up and tell them to their children,
> so that they should set their hope in God,
and not forget the works of God,
> but keep his commandments.

Glory to the Father . . .

SCRIPTURE   Wisdom 6:12-20
Wisdom is radiant and unfading,
and she is easily discerned by those who love her,
and is found by those who seek her.
She hastens to make herself known to those who desire her.
One who rises early to seek her will have no difficulty,
for she will be found sitting at the gate.
To fix one's thought on her is perfect understanding,
and one who is vigilant on her account will soon be free from
> care,
because she goes about seeking those worthy of her,
and she graciously appears to them in their paths,
and meets them in every thought.
The beginning of wisdom is the most sincere desire for instruction,
and concern for instruction is love of her,
and love of her is the keeping of her laws,
and giving heed to her laws is assurance of immortality,
and immortality brings one near to God;
so the desire for wisdom leads to a kingdom.

The Word of the Lord.

INTERCESSIONS

Wellspring of Life, you made us in your image to savor life and health. So we pray today for well-being, strength, and wisdom to pursue your justice in the world: *Just Lord, heal our troubled world and grant us peace.*

- Heal people who suffer from diseases and injuries of mind, body, and spirit. We pray to the Lord.
- Welcome into the joy of your eternal life those who will die today. We pray to the Lord.
- Bless those who minister to the sick and comfort the dying; grant them overflowing patience and compassion. We pray to the Lord.
- For what else shall we pray this morning? [Pause for participants to add their own intentions.] We pray to the Lord.

THE LORD'S PRAYER

With these petitions in our hearts, we pray as the Lord taught us: Our Father . . .

SHARING OF PEACE

CLOSING PRAYER

May God who is Ever-New bless the work of our hands and through our actions bestow well-being upon those we meet today. We ask this in Christ's name. AMEN.

THURSDAY EVENING

✝

Lord, teach us justice.
And we shall live in your peace.

PSALM 119:89-91, 102-105, 111-112
℟ People who practice justice, walk in the light of God.

The LORD exists forever;
    your word is firmly fixed in heaven.
Your faithfulness endures to all generations;
    you have established the earth, and it stands fast.
By your appointment they stand today,
    for all things are your servants. . . .

I do not turn away from your ordinances,
    for you have taught me.
How sweet are your words to my taste,
    sweeter than honey to my mouth!
Through your precepts I receive understanding;
    therefore I hate every false way.
Your word is a lamp to my feet
    and a light to my path. . . .

Your decrees are my heritage forever;
    they are the joy of my heart.
I incline my heart to perform your statutes
    forever, to the end.

Glory to the Father . . .

SCRIPTURE   John 21:15-17

When they had finished breakfast, Jesus said to Simon Peter, "Simon son of John, do you love me more than these?" He said to him, "Yes, Lord; you know that I love you." Jesus said to him, "Feed my lambs." A second time he said to him, "Simon son of John, do you love me?" He said to him, "Yes, Lord; you know that I love you." Jesus said to him, "Tend my sheep." He said to him the third time, "Simon son of John, do you love me?" Peter felt hurt because he said to him the third time, "Do you love me?" And he said to him, "Lord, you know everything; you know that I love you." Jesus said to him, "Feed my sheep."

The Gospel of the Lord.

SILENT REFLECTION

INTERCESSIONS

Life-giving Spirit, we are one people, yet divided by discord, illness, and fear, which sicken our lives together. And so we pray for health and well-being: *Just Lord, heal our troubled world and grant us peace.*

- Inspire leaders to secure the fundamental right of all human beings to good health. We pray to the Lord.
- Forgive us for neglecting those who are ailing; grant us healing hands to serve others. We pray to the Lord.
- Alleviate the suffering of those with illnesses of mind, body, or spirit, especially [pause for participants to add individual names or needs]. We pray to the Lord.

- For what else shall we pray because of our experiences today? [Pause for participants to add their own intentions.] We pray to the Lord.

THE LORD'S PRAYER
With these petitions in our hearts, we pray as the Lord taught us: Our Father . . .

SHARING OF PEACE

CLOSING PRAYER
May God who is Ever-New lead us into eternal life where all suffering will be wiped away. We ask this in Christ's name. AMEN.

FRIDAY MORNING

✝

Lord, teach us justice.
And we shall live in your peace.

PSALM 119:5-14
℟ People who practice justice, walk in the light of God.

O that my ways may be steadfast
   in keeping your statutes!
Then I shall not be put to shame,
   having my eyes fixed on all your commandments.
I will praise you with an upright heart,
   when I learn your righteous ordinances.
I will observe your statutes;
   do not utterly forsake me.

How can young people keep their way pure?
   By guarding it according to your word.
With my whole heart I seek you;
   do not let me stray from your commandments.
I treasure your word in my heart,
   so that I may not sin against you.
Blessed are you, O Lord;
   teach me your statutes.
With my lips I declare
   all the ordinances of your mouth.

I delight in the way of your decrees
as much as in all riches.

Glory to the Father . . .

SCRIPTURE   Sirach 14:20-26; 15:1-4

Happy is the person who meditates on wisdom
     and reasons intelligently,
who reflects in his heart on her ways
     and ponders her secrets,
pursuing her like a hunter,
     and lying in wait on her paths;
who peers through her windows
     and listens at her doors;
who camps near her house
     and fastens his tent peg to her walls;
who pitches his tent near her,
     and so occupies an excellent lodging place;
who places his children under her shelter,
     and lodges under her boughs. . . .

[W]hoever holds to the law will obtain wisdom.
She will come to meet him like a mother,
     and like a young bride she will welcome him.
She will feed him with the bread of learning,
     and give him the water of wisdom to drink.
He will lean on her and not fall,
     and he will rely on her and not be put to shame.

The Word of the Lord.

INTERCESSIONS

God of Compassion, Scripture reveals your tender love for us, like a mother who plays with a baby on her knee. Yet our societies often exploit people who have no one to protect them. So we pray today for them, your *anawim*: *Show us your mercy, O Lord.*

- Secure equal rights, responsibilities, and privileges for all women and girls throughout the world. We pray to the Lord.
- Protect the health and well-being of mothers, infants both born and unborn, and all children until their lives become a universal priority for every nation. We pray to the Lord.
- Teach women and men to respect each other as images of God, and to support each other in building just communities. We pray to the Lord.
- For what else shall we pray this morning? [Pause for participants to add their own intentions.] We pray to the Lord.

THE LORD'S PRAYER

With these petitions in our hearts, we pray as the Lord taught us: Our Father . . .

SHARING OF PEACE

CLOSING PRAYER

May God our Mother bless the work of our hands today and through our actions bring hope to the marginalized, especially the women and children we meet today. We ask this in Christ's name. AMEN.

FRIDAY EVENING

✝

Lord, teach us justice.
And we shall live in your peace.

PSALM 11
℟ People who practice justice, walk in the light of God.

In the LORD I take refuge; how can you say to me,
    "Flee like a bird to the mountains;
for look, the wicked bend the bow,
    they have fitted their arrow to the string,
    to shoot in the dark at the upright in heart.
If the foundations are destroyed,
    what can the righteous do?"

The LORD is in his holy temple;
    the LORD's throne is in heaven.
    His eyes behold, his gaze examines humankind.
The LORD tests the righteous and the wicked,
    and his soul hates the lover of violence.
On the wicked he will rain coals of fire and sulfur;
    a scorching wind shall be the portion of their cup.
For the LORD is righteous;
he loves righteous deeds;
    the upright shall behold his face.

Glory to the Father . . .

SCRIPTURE   John 4:7-10, 13-15

A Samaritan woman came to draw water, and Jesus said to her, "Give me a drink." (His disciples had gone to the city to buy food.) The Samaritan woman said to him, "How is it that you, a Jew, ask a drink of me, a woman of Samaria?" (Jews do not share things in common with Samaritans.) Jesus answered her, "If you knew the gift of God, and who it is that is saying to you, 'Give me a drink,' you would have asked him, and he would have given you living water." . . . [Then he] said to her, "Everyone who drinks of this water will be thirsty again, but those who drink of the water that I will give them will never be thirsty. The water that I will give will become in them a spring of water gushing up to eternal life." The woman said to him, "Sir, give me this water, so that I may never be thirsty or have to keep coming here to draw water."

The Gospel of the Lord.

SILENT REFLECTION

INTERCESSIONS

Spirit of Care, you hold us tenderly in your love. You alone can satisfy our thirst for justice and peace. And so we pray: *Show us your mercy, O Lord.*

- Grant leaders the wisdom to provide universal education, especially for women and girls, as a sure path to peace. We pray to the Lord.
- Forgive us for our contribution to systems that unjustly exclude women from full participation in society. We pray to the Lord.

- Protect women, children, and all others who live on the margins of life and community, especially [pause for participants to add individual names or needs]. We pray to the Lord.
- For what else shall we pray because of our experiences today? [Pause for participants to add their own intentions.] We pray to the Lord.

THE LORD'S PRAYER

With these petitions in our hearts, we pray as the Lord taught us: Our Father . . .

SHARING OF PEACE

CLOSING PRAYER

May God our Mother protect the vulnerable, awaken the privileged, and unite all women, children, and men into one community of peace. We ask this in Christ's name. AMEN.

SATURDAY MORNING

✝

Lord, teach us justice.
And we shall live in your peace.

PSALM 25:1-2, 4-6, 8-9, 12-13
℟ People who practice justice, walk in the light of God.

To you, O LORD, I lift up my soul.
O my God, in you I trust;
    do not let me be put to shame;
    do not let my enemies exult over me. . . .

Make me to know your ways, O LORD;
    teach me your paths.
Lead me in your truth, and teach me,
    for you are the God of my salvation;
    for you I wait all day long.

Be mindful of your mercy, O LORD, and of your steadfast love,
    for they have been from of old. . . .

Good and upright is the LORD;
    therefore he instructs sinners in the way.
He leads the humble in what is right,
    and teaches the humble his way. . . .

Who are they that fear the LORD?
    He will teach them the way that they should choose.

They will abide in prosperity,
    and their children shall possess the land.

Glory to the Father . . .

SCRIPTURE   Deuteronomy 4:1-2, 6-8
So now, Israel, give heed to the statutes and ordinances that I am teaching you to observe, so that you may live to enter and occupy the land that the LORD, the God of your ancestors, is giving you. You must neither add anything to what I command you nor take away anything from it, but keep the commandments of the LORD your God with which I am charging you. . . .

You must observe them diligently, for this will show your wisdom and discernment to the peoples, who, when they hear all these statutes, will say, "Surely this great nation is a wise and discerning people!" For what other great nation has a god so near to it as the LORD our God is whenever we call to him? And what other great nation has statutes and ordinances as just as this entire law that I am setting before you today?

The Word of the Lord.

INTERCESSIONS
God of Wisdom, we know that living with justice will bring us peace. So we pray today for wisdom to strive for a more equal distribution of property among nations and peoples in the world: *Lord, teach us to live justly.*

- Inspire leaders and lawmakers to provide education, employment, and dignified opportunities to satisfy the basic needs of all residents. We pray to the Lord.

- Restore the hope and dignity of people who experience exclusion due to race, social class, religion, ethnicity, or culture. We pray to the Lord.

- Teach us to follow the example of your Son, Jesus, so that we become more loving and compassionate to others. We pray to the Lord.

- For what else shall we pray this morning? [Pause for participants to add their own intentions.] We pray to the Lord.

THE LORD'S PRAYER

With these petitions in our hearts, we pray as the Lord taught us: Our Father . . .

SHARING OF PEACE

CLOSING PRAYER

May the God of Peace establish us in justice and, through our actions today, bring greater justice and peace to the people we encounter. We ask this in Christ's name. AMEN.

SATURDAY EVENING

✝

Lord, teach us justice.
And we shall live in your peace.

PSALM 103:6-8, 11-14
℟ People who practice justice, walk in the light of God.

The LORD works vindication
    and justice for all who are oppressed.
He made known his ways to Moses,
    his acts to the people of Israel.
The LORD is merciful and gracious,
    slow to anger and abounding in steadfast love. . . .

For as the heavens are high above the earth,
    so great is his steadfast love toward those who fear him;
as far as the east is from the west,
    so far he removes our transgressions from us.
As a father has compassion for his children,
    so the LORD has compassion for those who fear him.
For he knows how we were made;
    he remembers that we are dust.

Glory to the Father . . .

SCRIPTURE   John 6:3-13
Jesus went up the mountain and sat down there with his disciples. . . . When he looked up and saw a large crowd coming

toward him, Jesus said to Philip, "Where are we to buy bread for these people to eat?" He said this to test him, for he himself knew what he was going to do. Philip answered him, "Six months' wages would not buy enough bread for each of them to get a little." One of his disciples, Andrew, Simon Peter's brother, said to him, "There is a boy here who has five barley loaves and two fish. But what are they among so many people?" Jesus said, "Make the people sit down." Now there was a great deal of grass in the place; so they sat down, about five thousand in all. Then Jesus took the loaves, and when he had given thanks, he distributed them to those who were seated; so also the fish, as much as they wanted. When they were satisfied, he told his disciples, "Gather up the fragments left over, so that nothing may be lost." So they gathered them up, and from the fragments of the five barley loaves, left by those who had eaten, they filled twelve baskets.

The Gospel of the Lord.

SILENT REFLECTION

INTERCESSIONS

Spirit of Wisdom, you are the source of life, goodness, and plenty. Yet we fail to trust in your care and bounty. And so we pray for hearts filled with the trust that leads to justice: *Lord, teach us to live justly.*

- Grant all human beings greater appreciation for the connection between just communities and peaceful lives. We pray to the Lord.

- Renew the hope of people who thirst for justice so that they do not abandon the path that leads to peace. We pray to the Lord.
- Comfort and protect all people who suffer injustices at the hands of other human beings, especially [pause for participants to add individual names or needs]. We pray to the Lord.
- For what else shall we pray because of our experiences today? [Pause for participants to add their own intentions.] We pray to the Lord.

THE LORD'S PRAYER
With these petitions in our hearts, we pray as the Lord taught us:
Our Father . . .

SHARING OF PEACE

CLOSING PRAYER
May the God of Peace inspire us to practice justice and live in faithful service to the Gospel, until justice and peace are secured for all people. We ask this in Christ's name. AMEN.

Final Thoughts on the Command to Live Justly

This week's devotions invite us to reflect on the wisdom of justice. The readings emphasize that we ought to be just, as our God is just. We can reread the Scripture passages from this week, savor them, and make them our own. We might memorize a verse or imagine that we are present when Jesus teaches his disciples and feeds hungry crowds. As we recall our interactions this week, we can probe them by asking, Where do I find God's justice in my world? When I am just, what happens to me or to others who are involved?

Equally important, we are urged to make the connection between just communities and peace among people living there. Justice leads to peace because it safeguards the dignity of all people, including them fully in human society. Civil rights leader Martin Luther King Jr. said, "The arc of the moral universe is long, but it bends toward justice." His words testify to God's creation as a moral universe, where justice is the essence of God's command. King's words also remind us to stay faithful to the practice of justice, to have patience. Justice will bring peace; this is God's truth.

Still, when justice fails, the costs are heavy. Injustice hurts and we hear this in the cries of the poor. As we continue in the prayers of justice, we must share the lamentations of those who suffer when human beings refuse to live according to the justice God has ordained.

Week 2

INJUSTICE LAMENTED

Standing with Those Who Suffer Injustice

Just as God's command to human beings to live justly is ancient, so people's inhumanity to others is perennial. When justice fails in our world, there is suffering. This week's psalms and readings invite us to listen to the cries of those who suffer from injustice. Additionally, they oblige us to reflect on the distortions and privileges in our communities that cause conflict, misery, and anxiety.

Justice and injustice form a contrasting set. Justice serves the community by distributing goods fairly, by assuring all people participate in making decisions for their lives, and above all by treating people with dignity. Injustice destroys human relationships because only some have enough means to live on, only some have a say in governing their affairs, and not all are accorded respect and dignity. Where justice leads to peace and plenty, the harvest of injustice is suffering and distorted human lives.

Certainly, we experience natural pain during our lives. However, injustices such as poverty, violence, or discrimination intensify the daily challenge of securing basic needs. Injustice also causes its own sort of misery. Missing a lunch might be a trial, but hunger is unbearable when no nourishing food is available or there is no money to buy it. So we must notice that the poor, the marginalized, and those without power suffer the consequences of the sins of others. The chains of injustice, undeserved and unrelenting, bind them.

The psalms for this week resonate with sorrow, regret, loss, and lament. People cry to God from their profound and encompassing pain. They are circled by troubles, oppressed by evildoers, persecuted, and abandoned. The images of darkness, desolation, and despair summon our feelings of compassion and pity. In the Hebrew Scriptures, we also witness a poignant trust in God as redeemer and restorer. God responds tenderly, "O, afflicted one, storm-tossed, and not comforted" (Isa 54:11). God's love is steadfast and faithful; God will wipe away our tears. Finally, the gospel passages of evening devotions show Jesus sharing in human trials, as a refugee or one who is persecuted and cast out. Most importantly, they narrate Jesus' remarkable compassion as he heals the blind men and restores the widow's son.

God's promise, "I will never forget you," is fulfilled in Jesus. Yet we, as fellow human beings, are also called to have compassion and justice. The intercessions, therefore, focus on personal conversion so we learn to stand with victims of oppression. The intercessions compel us to recognize how injustice causes injury that reverberates across families and communities. In lamenting this week with those in trouble, we become attuned to the crying need for greater justice in our hearts and in our actions.

SUNDAY MORNING

✝

Lord, teach us justice.
And we shall live in your peace.

PSALM 86:1-3, 11-12, 14-15
℟ Console us, O Lord, and wipe away our tears.

Incline your ear, O LORD, and answer me,
    for I am poor and needy.
Preserve my life, for I am devoted to you;
    save your servant who trusts in you.
You are my God; be gracious to me, O Lord,
    for to you do I cry all day long. . . .

Teach me your way, O LORD,
    that I may walk in your truth;
    give me an undivided heart to revere your name.
I give thanks to you, O Lord my God, with my whole heart,
    and I will glorify your name forever. . . .

O God, the insolent rise up against me;
    a band of ruffians seeks my life,
    and they do not set you before them.
But you, O Lord, are a God merciful and gracious,
    slow to anger and abounding in steadfast love and faithfulness.

Glory to the Father . . .

SCRIPTURE   Isaiah 54:10-14

For the mountains may depart
   and the hills be removed,
but my steadfast love shall not depart from you,
   and my covenant of peace shall not be removed,
   says the LORD, who has compassion on you.

O afflicted one, storm-tossed, and not comforted,
   I am about to set your stones in [silver],
   and lay your foundations with sapphires.
I will make your pinnacles of rubies,
   your gates of jewels,
   and all your wall of precious stones.
All your children shall be taught by the LORD,
   and great shall be the prosperity of your children.
In righteousness you shall be established;
   you shall be far from oppression, for you shall not fear;
   and from terror, for it shall not come near you.

The Word of the Lord.

INTERCESSIONS

Compassionate God, your son Jesus Christ wept for your people who were storm-tossed and afflicted. Because you never abandon the least of your people, we have courage to pray: *Lord, open our hearts to the poor among us.*

- Save your people whose lives are diminished by lack of food, health, education, or community. We pray to the Lord.

- Teach us to reach out generously to those in need with permanent responses to restore to them dignity and self-respect. We pray to the Lord.

- Remind us of our own impoverishment, so we are moved to trust in your saving help. We pray to the Lord.

- For what else shall we pray this morning? [Pause for participants to add their own intentions.] We pray to the Lord.

THE LORD'S PRAYER
With these petitions in our hearts, we pray as the Lord taught us:
Our Father . . .

SHARING OF PEACE

CLOSING PRAYER
May the God of Solace open our eyes today to see the affliction of poverty, to understand its causes, and to work for its elimination. We ask this in Christ's name. AMEN.

SUNDAY EVENING

✝

Lord, teach us your justice.
And we shall live in your peace.

PSALM 71:1-4, 19-21
℟ Console us, O Lord, and wipe away our tears.

In you, O LORD, I take refuge;
    let me never be put to shame.
In your righteousness deliver me and rescue me;
    incline your ear to me and save me.
Be to me a rock of refuge,
    a strong fortress, to save me,
        for you are my rock and my fortress.

Rescue me, O my God, from the hand of the wicked,
    from the grasp of the unjust and cruel. . . .

Your power and your righteousness, O God,
    reach the high heavens.

You who have done great things,
    O God, who is like you?
You who have made me see many troubles and calamities
    will revive me again;
from the depths of the earth
    you will bring me up again.
You will increase my honor,
    and comfort me once again.

Glory to the Father . . .

SCRIPTURE   Luke 18:1-8

Then Jesus told them a parable about their need to pray always and not to lose heart. He said, "In a certain city there was a judge who neither feared God nor had respect for people. In that city there was a widow who kept coming to him and saying, 'Grant me justice against my opponent.' For a while he refused; but later he said to himself, 'Though I have no fear of God and no respect for anyone, yet because this widow keeps bothering me, I will grant her justice, so that she may not wear me out by continually coming.'" And the Lord said, "Listen to what the unjust judge says. And will not God grant justice to his chosen ones who cry to him day and night? Will he delay long in helping them? I tell you, he will quickly grant justice to them. And yet, when the Son of Man comes, will he find faith on earth?"

The Gospel of the Lord.

SILENT REFLECTION

INTERCESSIONS

Spirit of Compassion, help us to be ever mindful of the needs we have witnessed today. Teach us to remember the faces of our sisters and brothers suffering from want of any kind. And so we pray: *Lord, open our hearts to the poor among us.*

- Keep your suffering people from despair, until their needs are satisfied and their dignity restored. We pray to the Lord.
- Teach us to be trusted allies with the poor and persistent advocates for economic justice, until all people share justly in the bounty of creation. We pray to the Lord.

- Grant consolation and hope to all who experience destitution, especially [pause for participants to add individual names or needs]. We pray to the Lord.
- For what else shall we pray because of our experiences today? [Pause for participants to add their own intentions.] We pray to the Lord.

THE LORD'S PRAYER

With these petitions in our hearts, we pray as the Lord taught us:
Our Father . . .

SHARING OF PEACE

CLOSING PRAYER

May the God of Solace listen to the cries of the poor, come quickly to rescue those in need, and transform all nations into communities of justice and plenty. We ask this in Christ's name. AMEN.

MONDAY MORNING

✝

Lord, teach us justice.
And we shall live in your peace.

PSALM 31:1-5, 14-16
℞ Console us, O Lord, and wipe away our tears.

In you, O LORD, I seek refuge;
    do not let me ever be put to shame;
    in your righteousness deliver me.
Incline your ear to me;
    rescue me speedily.
Be a rock of refuge for me,
    a strong fortress to save me.

You are indeed my rock and my fortress;
    for your name's sake lead me and guide me,
take me out of the net that is hidden for me,
    for you are my refuge.
Into your hand I commit my spirit;
    you have redeemed me, O LORD, faithful God. . . .
I trust in you, O LORD;
    I say, "You are my God."
My times are in your hand;
    deliver me from the hand of my enemies and persecutors.

Let your face shine upon your servant;
　　save me in your steadfast love.

Glory to the Father . . .

SCRIPTURE　　　Habakkuk 1:2-4

O Lord, how long shall I cry for help,
　　and you will not listen?
Or cry to you "Violence!"
　　and you will not save?
Why do you make me see wrongdoing
　　and look at trouble?
Destruction and violence are before me;
　　strife and contention arise.
So the law becomes slack
　　and justice never prevails.
The wicked surround the righteous—
　　therefore judgment comes forth perverted.

The Word of the Lord.

INTERCESSIONS

God of Consolation, you hold in your tender love those people who must cope with the daily anguish of physical, emotional, and social violence. You weep for us in our strife and anguish. And so we turn to you for consolation and hope: *Lord, may peace reign in our hearts and in our lives.*

- Protect your people who live in fear of violence at the hands of other human beings. We pray to the Lord.

- Give us the courage and conviction to respond actively to end violence in our communities. We pray to the Lord.
- Bestow peace upon our world; bring a swift end to the wars and conflicts that divide people and nations. We pray to the Lord.
- For what else shall we pray this morning? [Pause for participants to add their own intentions.] We pray to the Lord.

THE LORD'S PRAYER
With these petitions in our hearts, we pray as the Lord taught us: Our Father . . .

SHARING OF PEACE

CLOSING PRAYER
May the God of Gentleness, the source of peace, show us how to build a world of secure and lasting peace. We ask this in Christ's name. AMEN.

MONDAY EVENING

✝

Lord, teach us your justice.
And we shall live in your peace.

PSALM 40:11-14, 16-17
R⁊ Console us, O Lord, and wipe away our tears.

Do not, O LORD, withhold
   your mercy from me;
let your steadfast love and your faithfulness
   keep me safe forever.
For evils have encompassed me
   without number;
my iniquities have overtaken me,
   until I cannot see;
they are more than the hairs of my head,
   and my heart fails me.
Be pleased, O LORD, to deliver me;
   O LORD, make haste to help me.
Let all those be put to shame and confusion
   who seek to snatch away my life;
let those be turned back and brought to dishonor
   who desire my hurt. . . .

But may all who seek you
   rejoice and be glad in you;
may those who love your salvation
   say continually, "Great is the LORD!"

As for me, I am poor and needy,
    but the Lord takes thought for me.
You are my help and my deliverer;
    do not delay, O my God.

Glory to the Father . . .

SCRIPTURE   Matthew 20:29-34
As they were leaving Jericho, a large crowd followed him. There
were two blind men sitting by the roadside. When they heard
that Jesus was passing by, they shouted, "Lord, have mercy on
us, Son of David!" The crowd sternly ordered them to be quiet;
but they shouted even more loudly, "Have mercy on us, Lord,
Son of David!" Jesus stood still and called them, saying, "What
do you want me to do for you?" They said to him, "Lord, let our
eyes be opened." Moved with compassion, Jesus touched their
eyes. Immediately they regained their sight and followed him.

The Gospel of the Lord.

SILENT REFLECTION

INTERCESSIONS
Spirit of Consolation, open our eyes and hearts to our sisters and
brothers who have been wounded by violence of any kind. And
so we pray: *Lord, may peace reign in our hearts, and in our lives.*

- Have mercy on those who suffer from injuries due to war
  and aggression; bring them to safety. We pray to the Lord.

- Protect and heal all children who are caught in conflicts that rage within their families, communities, and nations. We pray to the Lord.
- Bestow lasting joy on people who have suffered from violence and discord, especially [pause for participants to add individual names or needs]. We pray to the Lord.
- For what else shall we pray because of our experiences today? [Pause for participants to add their own intentions.] We pray to the Lord.

THE LORD'S PRAYER

With these petitions in our hearts, we pray as the Lord taught us: Our Father . . .

SHARING OF PEACE

CLOSING PRAYER

May the God of Gentleness, whose peace infinitely exceeds our imagination, forgive us for the times we have hurt others and fill the hearts of all people with lasting peace. We ask this in Christ's name. AMEN.

TUESDAY MORNING

✝

Lord, teach us justice.
And we shall live in your peace.

PSALM 16:1-9
℟ Console us, O Lord, and wipe away our tears.

Protect me, O God, for in you I take refuge.
I say to the LORD, "You are my Lord;
   I have no good apart from you."

As for the holy ones in the land, they are the noble,
   in whom is all my delight.

Those who choose another god multiply their sorrows;
   their drink offerings of blood I will not pour out
   or take their names upon my lips.

The LORD is my chosen portion and my cup;
   you hold my lot.
The boundary lines have fallen for me in pleasant places;
   I have a goodly heritage.
I bless the LORD who gives me counsel;
   in the night also my heart instructs me.
I keep the LORD always before me;
   because he is at my right hand, I shall not be moved.

Therefore my heart is glad, and my soul rejoices;
   my body also rests secure.

Glory to the Father . . .

SCRIPTURE   Lamentations 3:17-24, 31-33

[M]y soul is bereft of peace;
   I have forgotten what happiness is;
so I say, "Gone is my glory,
   and all that I had hoped for from the Lᴏʀᴅ."

The thought of my affliction and my homelessness
   is wormwood and gall!
My soul continually thinks of it
   and is bowed down within me.
But this I call to mind,
   and therefore I have hope:
The steadfast love of the Lᴏʀᴅ never ceases,
   his mercies never come to an end;
they are new every morning;
   great is your faithfulness.
"The Lᴏʀᴅ is my portion," says my soul,
   "therefore I will hope in him." . . .

For the Lord will not
   reject [his people] forever.
Although he causes grief, he will have compassion
   according to the abundance of his steadfast love;
for he does not willingly afflict
   or grieve anyone.

The Word of the Lord.

INTERCESSIONS

God of Enduring Mercy, you weep with those who are uprooted from their homes through no fault of their own. As your heart and hands, teach us to welcome immigrants into our community as friends and neighbors who bring blessings. And so we pray: *Lord, teach us to welcome each person who comes to us in need.*

- Swiftly reunite to their families children who have been separated from parents and relatives. We pray to the Lord.
- Heal refugees from their trauma and return them safely to their homes. We pray to the Lord.
- Inspire communities to offer welcome to immigrants far from their homelands and to value the varieties of culture, custom, and language. We pray to the Lord.
- For what else shall we pray this morning? [Pause for participants to add their own intentions.] We pray to the Lord.

THE LORD'S PRAYER

With these petitions in our hearts, we pray as the Lord taught us: Our Father . . .

SHARING OF PEACE

CLOSING PRAYER

May the God of Welcome open our hearts to all immigrants, refugees, and people who are far from home and family. We ask this in Christ's name. AMEN.

TUESDAY EVENING

✝

Lord, teach us your justice.
And we shall live in your peace.

PSALM 42:1-4, 9-11
℟ Console us, O Lord, and wipe away our tears.

As a deer longs for flowing streams,
    so my soul longs for you, O God.
My soul thirsts for God,
    for the living God.
When shall I come and behold
    the face of God?
My tears have been my food
    day and night,
while people say to me continually,
    "Where is your God?"

These things I remember,
    as I pour out my soul:
how I went with the throng,
    and led them in procession to the house of God,
with glad shouts and songs of thanksgiving,
    a multitude keeping festival. . . .

Why are you cast down, O my soul,
    and why are you disquieted within me?

Hope in God; for I shall again praise him,
   my help and my God.

Glory to the Father . . .

SCRIPTURE   Matthew 2:13-15, 19-23
Now after [the magi] had left, an angel of the Lord appeared to
Joseph in a dream and said, "Get up, take the child and his mother,
and flee to Egypt, and remain there until I tell you; for Herod is
about to search for the child, to destroy him." Then Joseph got
up, took the child and his mother by night, and went to Egypt,
and remained there until the death of Herod. This was to fulfill
what had been spoken by the Lord through the prophet, "Out of
Egypt I called my son." . . .

When Herod died, an angel of the Lord suddenly appeared in a
dream to Joseph in Egypt and said, "Get up, take the child and his
mother, and go to the land of Israel, for those who were seeking
the child's life are dead." Then Joseph got up, took the child and
his mother, and went to the land of Israel. But when he heard that
Archelaus was ruling over Judea in place of his father Herod, he
was afraid to go there. And after being warned in a dream, he
went away to the district of Galilee. There he made his home in
a town called Nazareth, so that what had been spoken through
the prophets might be fulfilled, "He will be called a Nazorean."

The Gospel of the Lord.

SILENT REFLECTION

INTERCESSIONS
Spirit of Enduring Mercy, show us how to create more hospitable communities for people who have joined us from afar. And so we pray: *Lord, teach us to welcome each person who comes to us in need.*

- End violence in every nation and return refugees to their homes to rebuild their lives. We pray to the Lord.
- Support people who have left home and family to seek a better life, and allow them to find safe shelter, dignified employment, and welcoming neighbors. We pray to the Lord.
- Protect travelers, immigrants, and all displaced people, especially [pause for participants to add individual names or needs]. We pray to the Lord.
- For what else shall we pray because of our experiences today? [Pause for participants to add their own intentions.] We pray to the Lord.

THE LORD'S PRAYER
With these petitions in our hearts, we pray as the Lord taught us: Our Father . . .

SHARING OF PEACE

CLOSING PRAYER
May the God of Welcome give courage to those who seek asylum and understanding hearts to those who shelter them. We ask this in Christ's name. AMEN.

WEDNESDAY MORNING

✝

Lord, teach us justice.
And we shall live in your peace.

PSALM 141:1-4, 8-10
℟ Console us, O Lord, and wipe away our tears.

I call upon you, O LORD; come quickly to me;
    give ear to my voice when I call to you.
Let my prayer be counted as incense before you,
    and the lifting up of my hands as an evening sacrifice.

Set a guard over my mouth, O LORD;
    keep watch over the door of my lips.
Do not turn my heart to any evil,
    to busy myself with wicked deeds
in company with those who work iniquity;
    do not let me eat of their delicacies. . . .

But my eyes are turned toward you, O GOD, my Lord;
    in you I seek refuge; do not leave me defenseless.
Keep me from the trap that they have laid for me,
    and from the snares of evildoers.
Let the wicked fall into their own nets,
    while I alone escape.

Glory to the Father . . .

SCRIPTURE   Jeremiah 14:2-5, 8-9

Judah mourns
    and her gates languish;
they lie in gloom on the ground,
    and the cry of Jerusalem goes up.
Her nobles send their servants for water;
    they come to the cisterns,
they find no water,
    they return with their vessels empty.
They are ashamed and dismayed
    and cover their heads,
because the ground is cracked.
    Because there has been no rain on the land
the farmers are dismayed;
    they cover their heads.
Even the doe in the field forsakes her newborn fawn
    because there is no grass. . . .
O hope of Israel,
    its savior in time of trouble,
why should you be like a stranger in the land,
    like a traveler turning aside for the night?
Why should you be like someone confused,
    like a mighty warrior who cannot give help?
Yet you, O Lord, are in the midst of us,
    and we are called by your name;
        do not forsake us!

The Word of the Lord.

INTERCESSIONS

Steadfast God, you gave us the earth as our common inheritance, yet so many are excluded from the riches of creation. Teach us to share the abundance of the earth more justly so that all people may know of your bounty. And so we pray: *Wellspring of Life, make us wise stewards of the earth and its blessings.*

- Increase our commitment to the environment and teach us to value ecological health above economic wealth. We pray to the Lord.

- Heal and protect people who suffer from chemical poisoning of their lands and homes. We pray to the Lord.

- Move us to assist communities destroyed by natural disasters to rebuild their lives. We pray to the Lord.

- For what else shall we pray this morning? [Pause for participants to add their own intentions.] We pray to the Lord.

THE LORD'S PRAYER

With these petitions in our hearts, we pray as the Lord taught us: Our Father . . .

SHARING OF PEACE

CLOSING PRAYER

May God, the Source of Life, make us mindful of our impact on the planet and on the well-being of others around the world. May we grow in our commitment to safeguard this planet for this generation and the next. We ask this in Christ's name. AMEN.

WEDNESDAY EVENING

✝

Lord, teach us your justice.
And we shall live in your peace.

PSALM 142:1-7
℞ Console us, O Lord, and wipe away our tears.

With my voice I cry to the LORD;
      with my voice I make supplication to the LORD.
I pour out my complaint before him;
      I tell my trouble before him.
When my spirit is faint,
      you know my way.

In the path where I walk
      they have hidden a trap for me.
Look on my right hand and see—
      there is no one who takes notice of me;
no refuge remains to me;
      no one cares for me.

I cry to you, O LORD;
      I say, "You are my refuge,
      my portion in the land of the living."
Give heed to my cry,
      for I am brought very low.

Save me from my persecutors,
      for they are too strong for me.

Bring me out of prison,
> so that I may give thanks to your name.
The righteous will surround me,
> for you will deal bountifully with me.

Glory to the Father . . .

SCRIPTURE   Luke 7:11-16
Soon afterwards [Jesus] went to a town called Nain, and his disciples and a large crowd went with him. As he approached the gate of the town, a man who had died was being carried out. He was his mother's only son, and she was a widow; and with her was a large crowd from the town. When the Lord saw her, he had compassion for her and said to her, "Do not weep." Then he came forward and touched the bier, and the bearers stood still. And he said, "Young man, I say to you, rise!" The dead man sat up and began to speak, and Jesus gave him to his mother. [Awe] seized all of them; and they glorified God, saying, "A great prophet has risen among us!" and "God has looked favorably on his people!"

The Word of the Lord.

SILENT REFLECTION

INTERCESSIONS
Steadfast Spirit, you sustain the hope of those who turn to you in times of crisis. Hear our prayers for a world in turmoil because we have failed to steward your gift. And so we pray: *Wellspring of Life, make us wise stewards of the earth and its blessings.*

- Bless those who have died because of humanity's abuse of the natural environment, and comfort those they have left behind. We pray to the Lord.

- Rouse nations and the international community to respond generously to protect the environment and restore its health. We pray to the Lord.

- Make us your hands and heart to safeguard people who suffer from storms, droughts, earthquakes, and other disasters of nature, especially [pause for participants to add individual names or needs]. We pray to the Lord.

- For what else shall we pray because of our experiences today? [Pause for participants to add their own intentions.] We pray to the Lord.

THE LORD'S PRAYER
With these petitions in our hearts, we pray as the Lord taught us:
Our Father . . .

SHARING OF PEACE

CLOSING PRAYER
May God, the Source of Life, bless and restore the earth and, through human efforts, secure its bounty for all people to share justly and fully. We ask this in Christ's name. AMEN.

THURSDAY MORNING

✝

Lord, teach us justice.
And we shall live in your peace.

PSALM 102:1-2, 6-12
℟ Console us, O Lord, and wipe away our tears.

Hear my prayer, O LORD;
    let my cry come to you.
Do not hide your face from me
    in the day of my distress.
Incline your ear to me;
    answer me speedily in the day when I call. . . .

I am like an owl of the wilderness,
        like a little owl of the waste places.
I lie awake;
    I am like a lonely bird on the housetop.
All day long my enemies taunt me;
    those who deride me use my name for a curse.
For I eat ashes like bread,
    and mingle tears with my drink,
because of your indignation and anger;
    for you have lifted me up and thrown me aside.
My days are like an evening shadow;
    I wither away like grass.

But you, O Lord, are enthroned forever;
   your name endures to all generations.

Glory to the Father . . .

SCRIPTURE   Judith 9:11-12, 14

"For your strength does not depend on numbers, nor your might on the powerful. But you are the God of the lowly, helper of the oppressed, upholder of the weak, protector of the forsaken, savior of those without hope. Please, please, God of my father, God of the heritage of Israel, Lord of heaven and earth, Creator of the waters, King of all your creation, hear my prayer! . . . Let your whole nation and every tribe know and understand that you are God, the God of all power and might, and that there is no other who protects the people of Israel but you alone!"

The Word of the Lord.

INTERCESSIONS

God of Deliverance, you created us to share life with you both now and eternally. Yet so many people despair and feel excluded from your love because their lives are plagued with diseases, sickness, and ill health. Knowing that you never abandon your people in their times of need, we pray: *Healing Lord, grant all your people health in body and spirit.*

- Strengthen health-care workers, caretakers, and all those who work in hospitals and clinics, that through their hands, people who are sick may be healed and comforted. We pray to the Lord.

- Save those who have no one to depend upon but you. We pray to the Lord.

- Inspire us to cultivate healthy individuals, healthy communities, and healthy nations. We pray to the Lord.

- For what else shall we pray this morning? [Pause for participants to add their own intentions.] We pray to the Lord.

THE LORD'S PRAYER
With these petitions in our hearts, we pray as the Lord taught us:
Our Father . . .

SHARING OF PEACE

CLOSING PRAYER
May God our Refuge heal the sick, refresh the weary, and deliver all people from harm on this new day of hope. We ask this in Christ's name. AMEN.

THURSDAY EVENING

✝

Lord, teach us your justice.
And we shall live in your peace.

PSALM 102:15-22, 28
℟ Console us, O Lord, and wipe away our tears.

The nations will fear the name of the LORD,
    and all the kings of the earth your glory.
For the LORD will build up Zion;
    he will appear in his glory.
He will regard the prayer of the destitute,
    and will not despise their prayer.

Let this be recorded for a generation to come,
    so that a people yet unborn may praise the LORD:
that he looked down from his holy height,
    from heaven the LORD looked at the earth,
to hear the groans of the prisoners,
    to set free those who were doomed to die;
so that the name of the LORD may be declared in Zion,
    and his praise in Jerusalem,
when peoples gather together,
    and kingdoms, to worship the LORD. . . .

The children of your servants shall live secure;
    their offspring shall be established in your presence.

Glory to the Father . . .

SCRIPTURE   Luke 17:11-19

On the way to Jerusalem Jesus was going through the region between Samaria and Galilee. As he entered a village, ten lepers approached him. Keeping their distance, they called out, saying, "Jesus, Master, have mercy on us!" When he saw them, he said to them, "Go and show yourselves to the priests." And as they went, they were made clean. Then one of them, when he saw that he was healed, turned back, praising God with a loud voice. He prostrated himself at Jesus' feet and thanked him. And he was a Samaritan. Then Jesus asked, "Were not ten made clean? But the other nine, where are they? Was none of them found to return and give praise to God except this foreigner?" Then he said to him, "Get up and go on your way; your faith has made you well."

The Gospel of the Lord.

SILENT REFLECTION

INTERCESSIONS

Spirit of Deliverance, Jesus cleansed the lepers, made the blind see and the lame walk. Now, as in every age, you are hope for people who are afflicted. And so we pray: *Healing Lord, grant all your people health in body and spirit.*

- Inspire us to advocate for health care for all people in our community. We pray to the Lord.

- Welcome into your loving presence those who will die today. We pray to the Lord.

- Give courage and hope to those who are sick, especially [pause for participants to add individual names or needs]. We pray to the Lord.

- For what else shall we pray because of our experiences today? [Pause for participants to add their own intentions.] We pray to the Lord.

THE LORD'S PRAYER

With these petitions in our hearts, we pray as the Lord taught us: Our Father . . .

SHARING OF PEACE

CLOSING PRAYER

May God our Refuge accompany all people who suffer this evening, holding them close with tender love and safeguarding them from despair. We ask this in Christ's name. AMEN.

FRIDAY MORNING

✝

Lord, teach us justice.
And we shall live in your peace.

PSALM 88:1-5, 13-14
℟ Console us, O Lord, and wipe away our tears.

O LORD, God of my salvation,
    when, at night, I cry out in your presence,
let my prayer come before you;
    incline your ear to my cry.

For my soul is full of troubles,
    and my life draws near to Sheol.
I am counted among those who go down to the Pit;
    I am like those who have no help,
like those forsaken among the dead,
    like the slain that lie in the grave,
like those whom you remember no more,
    for they are cut off from your hand. . . .

But I, O LORD, cry out to you;
    in the morning my prayer comes before you.
O LORD, why do you cast me off?
    Why do you hide your face from me?

Glory to the Father . . .

SCRIPTURE   Isaiah 49:8-11, 15-16

Thus says the Lord:

In a time of favor I have answered you,
    on a day of salvation I have helped you;
I have kept you and given you
    as a covenant to the people,
to establish the land,
    to apportion the desolate heritages;
saying to the prisoners, "Come out,"
    to those who are in darkness, "Show yourselves."
They shall feed along the ways,
    on all the bare heights shall be their pasture;
they shall not hunger or thirst,
    neither scorching wind nor sun shall strike them down,
for he who has pity on them will lead them,
    and by springs of water will guide them.
And I will turn all my mountains into a road,
    and my highways shall be raised up. . . .

Can a woman forget her nursing child,
    or show no compassion for the child of her womb?
Even these may forget,
    yet I will not forget you.
See, I have inscribed you on the palms of my hands.

The Word of the Lord.

INTERCESSIONS

God of Mercy, you are tender and compassionate to us in our needs. Yet we ourselves are often deaf and blind to people who are oppressed, especially women and children. And so we pray: *Show us your mercy, O Lord.*

- Empower women to support each other in every community, region, and nation as they struggle together for justice. We pray to the Lord.
- Come swiftly to protect women, children, and infants from physical, social, economic, and political injuries. We pray to the Lord.
- Unite all people to respect life and protect the young and the aged who are most vulnerable. We pray to the Lord.
- For what else shall we pray this morning? [Pause for participants to add their own intentions.] We pray to the Lord.

THE LORD'S PRAYER

With these petitions in our hearts, we pray as the Lord taught us: Our Father . . .

SHARING OF PEACE

CLOSING PRAYER

May God Emmanuel bless the work of our hands today and show us how to build communities where the dignity of all people is protected and honored. We ask this in Christ's name. AMEN.

FRIDAY EVENING

✝

Lord, teach us your justice.
And we shall live in your peace.

PSALM 13
℟ Console us, O Lord, and wipe away our tears.

How long, O LORD? Will you forget me forever?
　　How long will you hide your face from me?
How long must I bear pain in my soul,
　　and have sorrow in my heart all day long?
How long shall my enemy be exalted over me?

Consider and answer me, O LORD my God!
　　Give light to my eyes, or I will sleep the sleep of death,
and my enemy will say, "I have prevailed";
　　my foes will rejoice because I am shaken.

But I trusted in your steadfast love;
　　my heart shall rejoice in your salvation.
I will sing to the LORD,
　　because he has dealt bountifully with me.

Glory to the Father . . .

SCRIPTURE　　　Matthew 26:36-46
Then Jesus went with them to a place called Gethsemane; and
he said to his disciples, "Sit here while I go over there and pray."
He took with him Peter and the two sons of Zebedee, and began

to be grieved and agitated. Then he said to them, "I am deeply grieved, even to death; remain here, and stay awake with me." And going a little farther, he threw himself on the ground and prayed, "My Father, if it is possible, let this cup pass from me; yet not what I want but what you want." Then he came to the disciples and found them sleeping; and he said to Peter, "So, could you not stay awake with me one hour?" . . . Again he went away for the second time and prayed, "My Father, if this cannot pass unless I drink it, your will be done." Again he came and found them sleeping, . . . [so] he went away and prayed for the third time, saying the same words. Then he came to the disciples and said to them, "Are you still sleeping and taking your rest? . . . Get up, let us be going. See, my betrayer is at hand."

The Gospel of the Lord.

SILENT REFLECTION

INTERCESSIONS

Spirit of Mercy, you know our deepest despair when those we love and trust betray us, just as Jesus' companions betrayed him in the garden. And so we pray for a more steadfast commitment to the welfare of women, children, and all who depend upon us: *Show us your mercy, O Lord.*

- Make us watchful and alert to the impact of our choices on women, children, and families. We pray to the Lord.
- Transform our nations and communities to places where all people can share equally in the power, plenty, and privilege of society. We pray to the Lord.

- Protect all our sisters and brothers who seek shelter in your merciful care, especially [pause for participants to add individual names or needs]. We pray to the Lord.
- For what else shall we pray because of our experiences today? [Pause for participants to add their own intentions.] We pray to the Lord.

THE LORD'S PRAYER
With these petitions in our hearts, we pray as the Lord taught us: Our Father . . .

SHARING OF PEACE

CLOSING PRAYER
May God Emmanuel be gentle to us in our weakness and never forsake the least of our sisters and brothers. May God grant them comfort, hope, and repose. We ask this in Christ's name. AMEN.

SATURDAY MORNING

✠

Lord, teach us justice.
And we shall live in your peace.

PSALM 6:1-9
℟ Console us, O Lord, and wipe away our tears.

O Lord, do not rebuke me in your anger,
    or discipline me in your wrath.
Be gracious to me, O Lord, for I am languishing;
    O Lord, heal me, for my bones are shaking with terror.
My soul also is struck with terror,
    while you, O Lord—how long?

Turn, O Lord, save my life;
    deliver me for the sake of your steadfast love.
For in death there is no remembrance of you;
    in Sheol who can give you praise?

I am weary with my moaning;
    every night I flood my bed with tears;
    I drench my couch with my weeping.
My eyes waste away because of grief;
    they grow weak because of all my foes.

Depart from me, all you workers of evil,
    for the Lord has heard the sound of my weeping.

The LORD has heard my supplication;
    the LORD accepts my prayer.

Glory to the Father . . .

SCRIPTURE   Job 3:20-26

[Job lamented:] "Why is light given to one in misery,
    and life to the bitter in soul,
who long for death, but it does not come,
    and [who] dig for it more than for hidden treasures;
who rejoice exceedingly,
    and are glad when they find the grave?
Why is light given to one who cannot see the way,
    whom God has fenced in?
For my sighing comes like my bread,
    and my groanings are poured out like water.
Truly the thing that I fear comes upon me,
    and what I dread befalls me.
I am not at ease, nor am I quiet;
    I have no rest; but trouble comes.

The Word of the Lord.

INTERCESSIONS

God-for-us, many despair in life, like your servant Job. Let their cries reach our hearts. And so we pray: *Lord, teach us to live justly.*

- Soften our hearts and transform our priorities from individual self-sufficiency to responsible solidarity. We pray to the Lord.

- End human trafficking, all forms of slavery, and unjust imprisonment. We pray to the Lord.

- Grant people the grace and courage to stand together with those who are marginalized by their communities. We pray to the Lord.

- For what else shall we pray this morning? [Pause for participants to add their own intentions.] We pray to the Lord.

THE LORD'S PRAYER
With these petitions in our hearts, we pray as the Lord taught us:
Our Father . . .

SHARING OF PEACE

CLOSING PRAYER
May God our Redeemer hear our needs. Through God's grace, may we comfort people who suffer injustice and bring about a more humane world. We ask this in Christ's name. AMEN.

SATURDAY EVENING

✝

Lord, teach us your justice.
And we shall live in your peace.

PSALM 116:1-10
℟ Console us, O Lord, and wipe away our tears.

I love the LORD, because he has heard
   my voice and my supplications.
Because he inclined his ear to me,
   therefore I will call on him as long as I live.
The snares of death encompassed me;
   the pangs of Sheol laid hold on me;
   I suffered distress and anguish.
Then I called on the name of the LORD:
   "O LORD, I pray, save my life!"
Gracious is the LORD, and righteous;
   our God is merciful.
The LORD protects the simple;
   when I was brought low, he saved me.
Return, O my soul, to your rest,
   for the LORD has dealt bountifully with you.

For you have delivered my soul from death,
   my eyes from tears,
   my feet from stumbling.
I walk before the LORD
   in the land of the living.

I kept my faith, even when I said,
　"I am greatly afflicted."

Glory to the Father . . .

SCRIPTURE　　　Mark 5:25-34
Now there was a woman who had been suffering from hemorrhages for twelve years. She had endured much under many physicians, and had spent all that she had; and she was no better, but rather grew worse. She had heard about Jesus, and came up behind him in the crowd and touched his cloak, for she said, "If I but touch his clothes, I will be made well." Immediately her hemorrhage stopped; and she felt in her body that she was healed of her disease. Immediately aware that power had gone forth from him, Jesus turned about in the crowd and said, "Who touched my clothes?" . . . [The woman] came in fear and trembling, fell down before him, and told him the whole truth. He said to her, "Daughter, your faith has made you well; go in peace, and be healed of your disease."

The Gospel of the Lord.

SILENT REFLECTION

INTERCESSIONS
God-for-us, you created the world and showed us how to live justly. Our human injustices have caused suffering to many of our sisters and brothers. And so we pray: *Lord, teach us to live justly.*

- Inspire us to work for a more just distribution of wealth and power in the world. We pray to the Lord.
- Comfort those who are excluded from worldly goods, nourish their bodies and spirits, and give them true hope for a more just future. We pray to the Lord.
- Save all people who are experiencing injustice of any kind, especially [pause for participants to add individual names or needs]. We pray to the Lord.
- For what else shall we pray because of our experiences today? [Pause for participants to add their own intentions.] We pray to the Lord.

THE LORD'S PRAYER
With these petitions in our hearts, we pray as the Lord taught us:
Our Father . . .

SHARING OF PEACE

CLOSING PRAYER
May God our Redeemer save us. May God's justice rain down upon all women and men and wash away all our tears. We ask this in Christ's name. AMEN.

Final Thoughts on the Suffering Caused by Injustice

This week's prayer attempts to sharpen our awareness of how injustice impacts people who are most vulnerable. We can hear their lament—their sorrows, small and large. We realize that humanity is "a body of broken bones," as Merton describes us.*
In the psalm passages of this week, we hear some of the familiar psalms that speak of our most human condition—abandonment, sorrow, and loss. Lamenting injustice with those who suffer is an essential step toward a new order in the world.

Truly, the journey to wholeness requires a lifetime of compassionate action and honest reflection. So, we might listen attentively to those who are marginalized: What do they say they need? We can look for patterns of suffering: Where are our customs, practices, and laws biased in favor of power or privilege? When our gut yells, "It's not fair," we are obliged to question and probe this feeling: For whom is this unfair? What is justice in this place and time?

This week's lamentations shape our prayers and actions. In the next week, we renew our commitment to just action. Roused by the lamentations of human suffering, we are better prepared to stand with people abandoned and afflicted. As we begin to see the connection between injustice and suffering, we are better prepared to practice God's justice.

---

* Thomas Merton, *Seeds of Contemplation* (Norfolk, CT: New Directions, 1961), 72.

JUSTICE PRACTICED

Claiming Our Responsibility to Establish Justice

Our hearts have been opened to the tears of those who suffer from injustice in the world. The third week of the justice cycle now leads us along the path of repentance and continual conversion to stand with the marginalized. It is clear from God's commands and Jesus' example how we must live, but this new life of just action requires commitment. "Justice practiced" this week means exactly that: we must practice being just people if we want to live in a just society. Our hardened hearts are not replaced with human hearts overnight. Change requires God's grace as well as our willingness to live according to new values.

The themes in the readings for this week are repentance, reconciliation, and restoration. In the psalm selections, the struggle between justice and sinfulness comes to the fore. We hear this, for example, on Monday evening in Psalm 34: "Depart from evil, and do good; / seek peace, and pursue it." Other psalms voice God's faithfulness and steadfast justice. The readings from the Hebrew Scriptures speak of God's healing care for the earth and its inhabitants. God is bountiful, trustworthy, faithful, and compassionate. Yet God never cedes the essential commandment to humanity—we must act with justice and walk the path of peace. The gospel readings in the evenings complement the Hebrew

Scriptures. They describe Jesus' many miracles, when he healed the sick, fed the hungry, and ministered with compassion to the *anawim*, the least of human society. In addition to praying for God's intervention to help those in need, the intercessions repeatedly beg forgiveness for our failures and ask for grace in order to begin the serious practice of building a just society.

Taken together, the devotions urge us insistently to reflect on our own actions. Particularly important are the gospel passages where Jesus chastises people "of little faith" who fail to trust in God's just care. When we fail to trust God, we compete for "our share" of money, food, and comfort. Human competition, sparked by insecurity and greed, has ravaged societies since the dawn of civilization. Truly, we can say that failure to trust in God is the root of human injustice. Now, when we are reaching the earth's limit to satisfy our consumption-driven values, the need to pursue distributive and participatory justice is stark and urgent.

As we pray through this week, the morning and evening Offices again invite us to connect our actions with God's revelation. Practicing justice means acting, reflecting, evaluating, and deciding to renew our efforts. In the midst of the commitment to just practices, we hold fast to the truth that justice is the slow but sure path to peace for human communities. We trust in Jesus' promise that justice and compassion are light burdens and an easy yoke.

SUNDAY MORNING

✝

Lord, teach us justice.
And we shall live in your peace.

PSALM 41:1-6, 11-13
R̷ O God, in your mercy, call us back and convert our hearts.

Happy are those who consider the poor;
    the LORD delivers them in the day of trouble.
The LORD protects them and keeps them alive;
    they are called happy in the land.
      You do not give them up to the will of their enemies.
The LORD sustains them on their sickbed;
    in their illness you heal all their infirmities.

As for me, I said, "O LORD, be gracious to me;
    heal me, for I have sinned against you."
My enemies wonder in malice
    when I will die, and my name perish.
And when they come to see me, they utter empty words,
    while their hearts gather mischief;
      when they go out, they tell it abroad. . . .
By this I know that you are pleased with me;
    because my enemy has not triumphed over me.
But you have upheld me because of my integrity,
    and set me in your presence forever.

Blessed be the LORD, the God of Israel,
    from everlasting to everlasting.
Amen and Amen.

Glory to the Father . . .

SCRIPTURE   Isaiah 58:8-11
Then your light shall break forth like the dawn,
    and your healing shall spring up quickly;
your vindicator shall go before you,
    the glory of the LORD shall be your rear guard.
Then you shall call, and the LORD will answer;
    you shall cry for help, and he will say, Here I am.

If you remove the yoke from among you,
    the pointing of the finger, the speaking of evil,
if you offer your food to the hungry
    and satisfy the needs of the afflicted,
then your light shall rise in the darkness
    and your gloom be like the noonday.
The LORD will guide you continually,
    and satisfy your needs in parched places,
    and make your bones strong;
and you shall be like a watered garden,
    like a spring of water,
    whose waters never fail.

The Word of the Lord.

INTERCESSIONS
God of Hope, you judge our faithfulness to you by the way we
care for our sisters and brothers. Renew our commitment to the

common good so that no one will lack for food, shelter, safety, or employment. And so we pray: *Lord, open our hearts to the poor among us.*

- Convert our leaders to work for justice, creating more humane communities that serve the needs of all people. We pray to the Lord.
- Protect the poor from consequential injustices, such as diseases, violence, imprisonment, mental illness, and natural disasters. We pray to the Lord.
- Forgive us when we have placed our desire for luxuries above the needs of our brothers and sisters; change our hearts to feel their urgent pleas. We pray to the Lord.
- For what else shall we pray this morning? [Pause for participants to add their own intentions.] We pray to the Lord.

THE LORD'S PRAYER
With these petitions in our hearts, we pray as the Lord taught us: Our Father . . .

SHARING OF PEACE

CLOSING PRAYER
May the God of Forgiveness strengthen our resolve to work for justice and, through our actions, eliminate the poverty of our sisters and brothers. We ask this in Christ's name. AMEN.

SUNDAY EVENING

✟

Lord, teach us justice.
And we shall live in your peace.

PSALM 146:1-10
℟ O God, in your mercy, call us back and convert our hearts.

Praise the LORD!
Praise the LORD, O my soul!
I will praise the LORD as long as I live;
    I will sing praises to my God all my life long.

Do not put your trust in princes,
    in mortals, in whom there is no help.
When their breath departs, they return to the earth;
    on that very day their plans perish.

Happy are those whose help is the God of Jacob,
    whose hope is in the LORD their God,
who made heaven and earth,
    the sea, and all that is in them;
who keeps faith forever;
    who executes justice for the oppressed;
    who gives food to the hungry.

The LORD sets the prisoners free;
    the LORD opens the eyes of the blind.
The LORD lifts up those who are bowed down;
    the LORD loves the righteous.

The LORD watches over the strangers;
> he upholds the orphan and the widow,
> > but the way of the wicked he brings to ruin.
The LORD will reign forever,
> your God, O Zion, for all generations.
Praise the LORD!

Glory to the Father . . .

SCRIPTURE   Matthew 11:2-6

When John heard in prison what the Messiah was doing, he sent word by his disciples and said to him, "Are you the one who is to come, or are we to wait for another?" Jesus answered them, "Go and tell John what you hear and see: the blind receive their sight, the lame walk, the lepers are cleansed, the deaf hear, the dead are raised, and the poor have good news brought to them. And blessed is anyone who takes no offense at me."

The Gospel of the Lord.

SILENT REFLECTION

INTERCESSIONS

Spirit of Hope, again and again we have failed to live according to your just commands. In your mercy, forgive us once again, renew our trust in your saving care, and fill us with compassion. And so we pray: *Lord, open our hearts to the poor among us.*

- Humble our hard hearts and encourage us to live in solidarity with those who do not have enough. We pray to the Lord.

- Do not withhold your justice and send your Spirit to renew our broken communities without delay. We pray to the Lord.
- Hear the cry of the poor, especially [pause for participants to add individual names or needs]. We pray to the Lord.
- For what else shall we pray because of our experiences today? [Pause for participants to add their own intentions.] We pray to the Lord.

THE LORD'S PRAYER

With these petitions in our hearts, we pray as the Lord taught us: Our Father . . .

SHARING OF PEACE

CLOSING PRAYER

May the God of Forgiveness continue to heal the sick, feed the hungry, and care for the needs of all people, through our converted hearts and willing hands. We ask this in Christ's name. AMEN.

MONDAY MORNING

✝

Lord, teach us justice.
And we shall live in your peace.

PSALM 65:1-8
℟ O God, in your mercy, call us back and convert our hearts.

Praise is due to you,
   O God, in Zion;
and to you shall vows be performed,
O you who answer prayer!
   To you all flesh shall come.
When deeds of iniquity overwhelm us,
   you forgive our transgressions.

Happy are those whom you choose and bring near
   to live in your courts.
We shall be satisfied with the goodness of your house,
   your holy temple.

By awesome deeds you answer us with deliverance,
   O God of our salvation;
you are the hope of all the ends of the earth
   and of the farthest seas.

By your strength you established the mountains;
   you are girded with might.

You silence the roaring of the seas,
    the roaring of their waves,
    the tumult of the peoples.
Those who live at earth's farthest bounds are awed by your signs;
you make the gateways of the morning and the evening shout
       for joy.

Glory to the Father . . .

SCRIPTURE   Ezekiel 36:26-28, 33-35

A new heart I will give you, and a new spirit I will put within you; and I will remove from your body the heart of stone and give you a heart of flesh. I will put my spirit within you, and make you follow my statutes and be careful to observe my ordinances. Then you shall live in the land that I gave to your ancestors; and you shall be my people, and I will be your God. . . . On the day that I cleanse you from all your iniquities, I will cause the towns to be inhabited, and the waste places shall be rebuilt. The land that was desolate shall be tilled, instead of being the desolation that it was in the sight of all who passed by. And they will say, "This land that was desolate has become like the garden of Eden."

The Word of the Lord.

INTERCESSIONS

God of Rebirth, heal the hearts of the desolate and weary; lead us along the path of justice to peace. And so we pray: *Lord, may peace reign in our hearts and in our lives.*

- Forgive us for the violence we have committed and the wars that have been waged in our name. We pray to the Lord.

- Bless children everywhere with an understanding of peace, so that future generations may strive more urgently to build a just world. We pray to the Lord.

- Protect from harm all people who live in areas of active conflict, especially [pause for participants to add their own intentions]. We pray to the Lord.

- For what else shall we pray this morning? [Pause for participants to add their own intentions.] We pray to the Lord.

THE LORD'S PRAYER
With these petitions in our hearts, we pray as the Lord taught us: Our Father . . .

SHARING OF PEACE

CLOSING PRAYER
May the God of Peace move us to convert our weapons of violence into tools for life and peace. We ask this in Christ's name. AMEN.

MONDAY EVENING

✝

Lord, teach us justice.
And we shall live in your peace.

PSALM 34:4-5, 8-9, 14-18
℟ O God, in your mercy, call us back and convert our hearts.

I sought the LORD, and he answered me,
    and delivered me from all my fears.
Look to him, and be radiant;
    so your faces shall never be ashamed. . . .

O taste and see that the LORD is good;
    happy are those who take refuge in him.
O fear the LORD, you his holy ones,
    for those who fear him have no want. . . .

Depart from evil, and do good;
    seek peace, and pursue it.
The eyes of the LORD are on the righteous,
    and his ears are open to their cry.
The face of the LORD is against evildoers,
    to cut off the remembrance of them from the earth.
When the righteous cry for help, the LORD hears,
    and rescues them from all their troubles.
The LORD is near to the brokenhearted,
    and saves the crushed in spirit.

Glory to the Father . . .

SCRIPTURE   Matthew 6:25-30

[Jesus said to them:] "Therefore I tell you, do not worry about your life, what you will eat or what you will drink, or about your body, what you will wear. Is not life more than food, and the body more than clothing? Look at the birds of the air; they neither sow nor reap nor gather into barns, and yet your heavenly Father feeds them. Are you not of more value than they? And can any of you by worrying add a single hour to your span of life? And why do you worry about clothing? Consider the lilies of the field, how they grow; they neither toil nor spin, yet I tell you, even Solomon in all his glory was not clothed like one of these. But if God so clothes the grass of the field, which is alive today and tomorrow is thrown into the oven, will he not much more clothe you—you of little faith?"

The Gospel of the Lord.

SILENT REFLECTION

INTERCESSIONS

Spirit of Rebirth, rouse us to protect people who are victims of violence and not to relent until all are able to live in security. And so, trusting where you lead us, we pray: *Lord, may peace reign in our hearts and in our lives.*

- Bless those who practice nonviolence and allow their witness to inspire others. We pray to the Lord.
- Welcome into your presence those who have died in wars or through violence of any kind. We pray to the Lord.

- Reestablish peace and safety in human communities everywhere and protect all human life, especially [pause for participants to add individual names or needs]. We pray to the Lord.

- For what else shall we pray because of our experiences today? [Pause for participants to add their own intentions.] We pray to the Lord.

THE LORD'S PRAYER
With these petitions in our hearts, we pray as the Lord taught us:
Our Father . . .

SHARING OF PEACE

CLOSING PRAYER
May the God of Peace bestow tranquility upon every nation and community so that all people will enjoy lives of safety and security. We ask this in Christ's name. AMEN.

TUESDAY MORNING

✝

Lord, teach us justice.
And we shall live in your peace.

PSALM 111:1-10
℟ O God, in your mercy, call us back and convert our hearts.

Praise the LORD!
I will give thanks to the LORD with my whole heart,
    in the company of the upright, in the congregation.
Great are the works of the LORD,
    studied by all who delight in them.
Full of honor and majesty is his work,
    and his righteousness endures forever.
He has gained renown by his wonderful deeds;
    the LORD is gracious and merciful.
He provides food for those who fear him;
    he is ever mindful of his covenant.
He has shown his people the power of his works,
    in giving them the heritage of the nations.
The works of his hands are faithful and just;
    all his precepts are trustworthy.
They are established forever and ever,
    to be performed with faithfulness and uprightness.

He sent redemption to his people;
    he has commanded his covenant forever.
    Holy and awesome is his name.
The fear of the LORD is the beginning of wisdom;
    all those who practice wisdom have a good understanding.
    His praise endures forever.

Glory to the Father . . .

SCRIPTURE   Zechariah 7:4-10

Then the word of the LORD of hosts came to me: Say to all the people of the land and the priests: When you fasted and lamented in the fifth month and in the seventh, for these seventy years, was it for me that you fasted? And when you eat and when you drink, do you not eat and drink only for yourselves? Were not these the words that the LORD proclaimed by the former prophets, when Jerusalem was inhabited and in prosperity, along with the towns around it, and when the Negeb and the Shephelah were inhabited?

The word of the LORD came to Zechariah, saying: Thus says the LORD of hosts: Render true judgments, show kindness and mercy to one another; do not oppress the widow, the orphan, the alien, or the poor; and do not devise evil in your hearts against one another.

The Word of the Lord.

INTERCESSIONS

Sheltering God, in our global society, many people travel far from home seeking jobs, safety, and better lives for their families. You have commanded us to welcome and safeguard them. And so we pray: *Lord, teach us to welcome each person who comes to us in need.*

- Motivate us to share our resources willingly with refugees trying to find their families and return to their homes. We pray to the Lord.
- Protect those who have crossed borders seeking a place to live where they can be safe from harm. We pray to the Lord.
- Inspire our legislators, leaders, and citizens to defend the dignity of all people who come to our nation for sanctuary. We pray to the Lord.
- For what else shall we pray this morning? [Pause for participants to add their own intentions.] We pray to the Lord.

THE LORD'S PRAYER

With these petitions in our hearts, we pray as the Lord taught us: Our Father . . .

SHARING OF PEACE

CLOSING PRAYER

God of Justice, arouse our compassion for people seeking asylum and protection, when we recall the times we have been strangers, lost and alone. We ask this in Christ's name. AMEN.

TUESDAY EVENING

✝

Lord, teach us justice.
And we shall live in your peace.

PSALM 71:1-2, 12-16
R/ O God, in your mercy, call us back and convert our hearts.

In you, O LORD, I take refuge;
  let me never be put to shame.
In your righteousness deliver me and rescue me;
  incline your ear to me and save me. . . .

O God, do not be far from me;
  O my God, make haste to help me!
Let my accusers be put to shame and consumed;
  let those who seek to hurt me
  be covered with scorn and disgrace.
But I will hope continually,
  and will praise you yet more and more.
My mouth will tell of your righteous acts,
  of your deeds of salvation all day long,
  though their number is past my knowledge.
I will come praising the mighty deeds of the Lord GOD,
  I will praise your righteousness, yours alone.

Glory to the Father . . .

SCRIPTURE   John 8:3-11
The scribes and the Pharisees brought a woman who had been
caught in adultery; and making her stand before all of them,

they said to him, "Teacher, this woman was caught in the very act of committing adultery. Now in the law Moses commanded us to stone such women. Now what do you say?" They said this to test him, so that they might have some charge to bring against him. Jesus bent down and wrote with his finger on the ground. When they kept on questioning him, he straightened up and said to them, "Let anyone among you who is without sin be the first to throw a stone at her." And once again he bent down and wrote on the ground. When they heard it, they went away, one by one, beginning with the elders; and Jesus was left alone with the woman standing before him. Jesus straightened up and said to her, "Woman, where are they? Has no one condemned you?" She said, "No one, sir." And Jesus said, "Neither do I condemn you. Go your way, and from now on do not sin again."

The Gospel of the Lord.

SILENT REFLECTION

INTERCESSIONS
Sheltering Spirit, all who seek your protection find hope. Forgive us when we have failed to embrace people in need. And so we pray: *Lord, teach us to welcome each person who comes to us in need.*

- Welcome into your presence those who have died striving for a better life for themselves and their families. We pray to the Lord.
- Rouse our governments locally, nationally, and internationally to pass laws to protect refugees and restore their communities. We pray to the Lord.

- Comfort everyone who experiences alienation and isolation, especially [pause for participants to add individual names or needs]. We pray to the Lord.

- For what else shall we pray because of our experiences today? [Pause for participants to add their own intentions.] We pray to the Lord.

THE LORD'S PRAYER
With these petitions in our hearts, we pray as the Lord taught us:
Our Father . . .

SHARING OF PEACE

CLOSING PRAYER
May the God of Justice help people everywhere to recognize their common needs and desires, so that we can live together in solidarity as one community of peace. We ask this in Christ's name. AMEN.

WEDNESDAY MORNING

✝

Lord, teach us justice.
And we shall live in your peace.

PSALM 68:4-10
℟ O God, in your mercy, call us back and convert our hearts.

Sing to God, sing praises to his name;
    lift up a song to him who rides upon the clouds—
his name is the LORD—
    be exultant before him.

Father of orphans and protector of widows
    is God in his holy habitation.
God gives the desolate a home to live in;
    he leads out the prisoners to prosperity,
    but the rebellious live in a parched land.

O God, when you went out before your people,
    when you marched through the wilderness,
the earth quaked, the heavens poured down rain
    at the presence of God, the God of Sinai,
    at the presence of God, the God of Israel.
Rain in abundance, O God, you showered abroad;
    you restored your heritage when it languished;

your flock found a dwelling in it;
in your goodness, O God, you provided for the needy.

Glory to the Father . . .

SCRIPTURE   Leviticus 26:2-6
You shall keep my sabbaths and reverence my sanctuary: I am the LORD.

If you follow my statutes and keep my commandments and observe them faithfully, I will give you your rains in their season, and the land shall yield its produce, and the trees of the field shall yield their fruit. Your threshing shall overtake the vintage, and the vintage shall overtake the sowing; you shall eat your bread to the full, and live securely in your land. And I will grant peace in the land, and you shall lie down, and no one shall make you afraid; I will remove dangerous animals from the land, and no sword shall go through your land.

The Word of the Lord.

INTERCESSIONS
God of Abundance, we recognize that the poor are especially vulnerable to the damage human beings have caused to the environment. They are powerless to oppose the pollution of their air, land, and water. And so we pray: *Wellspring of Life, make us wise stewards of the earth and its blessings.*

- Make us recognize the interdependence of all human communities and give us the willingness to act in solidarity with the earth. We pray to the Lord.

- Inspire governments and other organizations to act swiftly to assure their needs of those who lack clean water and air. We pray to the Lord.

- Help us to protect the well-being of all other species who inhabit the earth with us. We pray to the Lord.

- For what else shall we pray this morning? [Pause for participants to add their own intentions.] We pray to the Lord.

THE LORD'S PRAYER

With these petitions in our hearts, we pray as the Lord taught us: Our Father . . .

SHARING OF PEACE

CLOSING PRAYER

May the Creator of Life instill in us a sacred appreciation for the world around us and an unwavering desire to safeguard life in all its diversity. We ask this in Christ's name. AMEN.

WEDNESDAY EVENING

✝

Lord, teach us justice.
And we shall live in your peace.

PSALM 107:35-43
℟ O God, in your mercy, call us back and convert our hearts.

[The Lord] turns a desert into pools of water,
    a parched land into springs of water.
And there he lets the hungry live,
    and they establish a town to live in;
they sow fields, and plant vineyards,
    and get a fruitful yield.
By his blessing they multiply greatly,
    and he does not let their cattle decrease.

When they are diminished and brought low
    through oppression, trouble, and sorrow,
he pours contempt on princes
    and makes them wander in trackless wastes;
but he raises up the needy out of distress,
    and makes their families like flocks.
The upright see it and are glad;
    and all wickedness stops its mouth.
Let those who are wise give heed to these things,
    and consider the steadfast love of the LORD.

Glory to the Father . . .

SCRIPTURE   Luke 6:27-31, 37-38

"But I say to you that listen, Love your enemies, do good to those who hate you, bless those who curse you, pray for those who abuse you. If anyone strikes you on the cheek, offer the other also; and from anyone who takes away your coat do not withhold even your shirt. Give to everyone who begs from you; and if anyone takes away your goods, do not ask for them again. Do to others as you would have them do to you. . . . Do not judge, and you will not be judged; do not condemn, and you will not be condemned. Forgive, and you will be forgiven; give, and it will be given to you. A good measure, pressed down, shaken together, running over, will be put into your lap; for the measure you give will be the measure you get back."

The Gospel of the Lord.

SILENT REFLECTION

INTERCESSIONS

Spirit of Abundance, we humbly acknowledge the way we have so often used up your creation without regard to replenishing and restoring what we have taken. And so we pray: *Wellspring of Life, make us wise stewards of the earth and its blessings.*

- Forgive our wasteful habits; show us how to live more simply. We pray to the Lord.

- Bestow your abundant life on the waters, the fields, and the air to heal them and restore them to fruitfulness. We pray to the Lord.

- Grant all your people safe natural environments, especially [pause for participants to add individual names or needs]. We pray to the Lord.
- For what else shall we pray because of our experiences today? [Pause for participants to add their own intentions.] We pray to the Lord.

THE LORD'S PRAYER
With these petitions in our hearts, we pray as the Lord taught us: Our Father . . .

SHARING OF PEACE

CLOSING PRAYER
May the God of Abundance multiply our work to create more just and sustainable human communities. We ask this in Christ's name. AMEN.

THURSDAY MORNING

✝

Lord, teach us justice.
And we shall live in your peace.

PSALM 107:1-3, 17-22
℟ O God, in your mercy, call us back and convert our hearts.

O give thanks to the LORD, for he is good;
    for his steadfast love endures forever.
Let the redeemed of the LORD say so,
    those he redeemed from trouble
and gathered in from the lands,
    from the east and from the west,
    from the north and from the south. . . .

Some were sick through their sinful ways,
    and because of their iniquities endured affliction;
they loathed any kind of food,
    and they drew near to the gates of death.
Then they cried to the LORD in their trouble,
    and he saved them from their distress;
he sent out his word and healed them,
    and delivered them from destruction.
Let them thank the LORD for his steadfast love,
    for his wonderful works to humankind.

And let them offer thanksgiving sacrifices,
and tell of his deeds with songs of joy.

Glory to the Father . . .

SCRIPTURE   Isaiah 40:27-31
Why do you say, O Jacob,
and speak, O Israel,
"My way is hidden from the LORD,
and my right is disregarded by my God"?
Have you not known? Have you not heard?
The LORD is the everlasting God,
the Creator of the ends of the earth.
He does not faint or grow weary;
his understanding is unsearchable.
He gives power to the faint,
and strengthens the powerless.
Even youths will faint and be weary,
and the young will fall exhausted;
but those who wait for the LORD shall renew their strength,
they shall mount up with wings like eagles,
they shall run and not be weary,
they shall walk and not faint.

The Word of the Lord.

INTERCESSIONS
God of Life, you count all your children sacred and number us
among the stars. You delight in our well-being like a parent en-
joying a child at play. And so we pray today: *Just Lord, heal our
troubled world and grant us peace.*

- Forgive us when we have been indifferent to the well-being of others; make us compassionate toward those who suffer. We pray to the Lord.

- Move the international community to secure basic medical care for all people around the world. We pray to the Lord.

- Give strength to children who are weak and weary; restore them so that they may enjoy life in its abundance. We pray to the Lord.

- For what else shall we pray this morning? [Pause for participants to add their own intentions.] We pray to the Lord.

THE LORD'S PRAYER
With these petitions in our hearts, we pray as the Lord taught us: Our Father . . .

SHARING OF PEACE

CLOSING PRAYER
May the God who protects the humble use our hearts and hands to heal the ailing world and establish justice by our actions. We ask this in Christ's name. AMEN.

THURSDAY EVENING

✝

Lord, teach us justice.
And we shall live in your peace.

PSALM 145:9-10, 14-18
R⁊ O God, in your mercy, call us back and convert our hearts.

The LORD is good to all,
    and his compassion is over all that he has made.

All your works shall give thanks to you, O LORD,
    and all your faithful shall bless you. . . .

The LORD upholds all who are falling,
    and raises up all who are bowed down.
The eyes of all look to you,
    and you give them their food in due season.
You open your hand,
    satisfying the desire of every living thing.
The LORD is just in all his ways,
    and kind in all his doings.
The LORD is near to all who call on him,
    to all who call on him in truth.

Glory to the Father . . .

SCRIPTURE   Luke 4:16-22
When [Jesus] came to Nazareth, where he had been brought up,
he went to the synagogue on the sabbath day, as was his custom.

He stood up to read, and the scroll of the prophet Isaiah was given to him. He unrolled the scroll and found the place where it was written:

> "The Spirit of the Lord is upon me,
>   because he has anointed me
>   to bring good news to the poor.
> He has sent me to proclaim release to the captives
>   and recovery of sight to the blind,
>   to let the oppressed go free,
> to proclaim the year of the Lord's favor."

And he rolled up the scroll, gave it back to the attendant, and sat down. The eyes of all in the synagogue were fixed on him. Then he began to say to them, "Today this scripture has been fulfilled in your hearing." All spoke well of him and were amazed at the gracious words that came from his mouth.

The Gospel of the Lord.

SILENT REFLECTION

INTERCESSIONS
Spirit of Life, Jesus Christ proclaimed the good news of your favor for those in need. And so we have the confidence to pray: *Just Lord, heal our troubled world and grant us peace.*

- Remove from our hearts the fear, ignorance, and insensitivity that keep us from caring fully for the needs of others. We pray to the Lord.

- Teach us to understand community health as a matter of justice, which we can address through human commitment. We pray to the Lord.

- Heal your people who are sick, comfort those who are dying, and give strength to all who care for those in need, especially [pause for participants to add individual names or needs]. We pray to the Lord.

- For what else shall we pray because of our experiences today? [Pause for participants to add their own intentions.] We pray to the Lord.

THE LORD'S PRAYER
With these petitions in our hearts, we pray as the Lord taught us: Our Father . . .

SHARING OF PEACE

CLOSING PRAYER
May the God who protects the humble teach us to treasure life and health, to comfort those who are ill, and to build communities where all people can flourish. We ask this in Christ's name. AMEN.

FRIDAY MORNING

✝

Lord, teach us justice.
And we shall live in your peace.

PSALM 51:1-6, 13, 15-17
℟ O God, in your mercy, call us back and convert our hearts.

Have mercy on me, O God,
    according to your steadfast love;
according to your abundant mercy
    blot out my transgressions.
Wash me thoroughly from my iniquity,
    and cleanse me from my sin.

For I know my transgressions,
    and my sin is ever before me.
Against you, you alone, have I sinned,
    and done what is evil in your sight,
so that you are justified in your sentence
    and blameless when you pass judgment.
Indeed, I was born guilty,
    a sinner when my mother conceived me.
You desire truth in the inward being;
    therefore teach me wisdom in my secret heart. . . .

Then I will teach transgressors your ways,
    and sinners will return to you. . . .

O Lord, open my lips,
    and my mouth will declare your praise.
For you have no delight in sacrifice;
    if I were to give a burnt offering, you would not be pleased.
The sacrifice acceptable to God is a broken spirit;
    a broken and contrite heart, O God, you will not despise.

Glory to the Father . . .

SCRIPTURE   Hosea 11:3-4, 8-11
Yet it was I who taught Ephraim to walk,
    I took them up in my arms;
        but they did not know that I healed them.
I led them with cords of human kindness,
    with bands of love.
I was to them like those
    who lift infants to their cheeks.
        I bent down to them and fed them. . . .

How can I give you up, Ephraim?
    How can I hand you over, O Israel? . . .
My heart recoils within me;
    my compassion grows warm and tender.
I will not execute my fierce anger;
    I will not again destroy Ephraim;
for I am God and no mortal,
    the Holy One in your midst,
    and I will not come in wrath.

They shall go after the LORD,
    who roars like a lion;

when he roars,
    his children shall come trembling from the west.
They shall come trembling like birds from Egypt,
    and like doves from the land of Assyria;
    and I will return them to their homes, says the LORD.

The Word of the Lord.

INTERCESSIONS

God of Forgiveness, you love us intimately and tenderly. Spare your wrath and instead inspire us to imitate your tenderness to those without power or means. And so we pray for all your children: *Show us your mercy, O Lord.*

- Strengthen all nations' resolve to secure full political rights, responsibilities, and privileges for women. We pray to the Lord.

- Safeguard the lives and health of women and children and give us the courage to stand in solidarity with them. We pray to the Lord.

- Inspire women and men together to respect and support each other as distinctive images of your loving care. We pray to the Lord.

- For what else shall we pray this morning? [Pause for participants to add their own intentions.] We pray to the Lord.

THE LORD'S PRAYER

With these petitions in our hearts, we pray as the Lord taught us: Our Father . . .

SHARING OF PEACE

CLOSING PRAYER
May the God of Love open our minds and hearts to accept all people as full members of one worldwide human community. We ask this in Christ's name. AMEN.

FRIDAY EVENING

Lord, teach us justice.
And we shall live in your peace.

PSALM 40:6-11
℟ O God, in your mercy, call us back and convert our hearts.

Sacrifice and offering you do not desire,
    but you have given me an open ear.
Burnt offering and sin offering
    you have not required.
Then I said, "Here I am;
    in the scroll of the book it is written of me.
I delight to do your will, O my God;
    your law is within my heart."

I have told the glad news of deliverance
    in the great congregation;
see, I have not restrained my lips,
    as you know, O Lord.
I have not hidden your saving help within my heart,
    I have spoken of your faithfulness and your salvation;
I have not concealed your steadfast love and your faithfulness
    from the great congregation.

Do not, O Lord, withhold
    your mercy from me;

let your steadfast love and your faithfulness
    keep me safe forever.

Glory to the Father . . .

SCRIPTURE   Luke 19:1-10

[Jesus] entered Jericho and was passing through it. A man was there named Zacchaeus; he was a chief tax collector and was rich. He was trying to see who Jesus was, but on account of the crowd he could not, because he was short in stature. So he ran ahead and climbed a sycamore tree to see him . . . When Jesus came to the place, he looked up and said to him, "Zacchaeus, hurry and come down; for I must stay at your house today." So he hurried down and was happy to welcome him. All who saw it began to grumble and said, "He has gone to be the guest of one who is a sinner." Zacchaeus stood there and said to the Lord, "Look, half of my possessions, Lord, I will give to the poor; and if I have defrauded anyone of anything, I will pay back four times as much." Then Jesus said to him, "Today salvation has come to this house, because he too is a son of Abraham. For the Son of Man came to seek out and to save the lost."

The Gospel of the Lord.

SILENT REFLECTION

INTERCESSIONS

Spirit of Forgiveness, you continually call us back to the path of justice and righteousness. Like Zacchaeus the tax collector, make us mindful that our failures injure others and make us willing to rectify oppression: *Show us your mercy, O Lord.*

- Bless and comfort those people who live at the margins of society, without power or voice, especially women and children. We pray to the Lord.

- Inspire all nations to extend full political rights to women and to make them full participants in determining their futures. We pray to the Lord.

- Hold in your special care women and children who have suffered due to their vulnerability and powerlessness, especially [pause for participants to add individual names or needs]. We pray to the Lord.

- For what else shall we pray because of our experiences today? [Pause for participants to add their own intentions.] We pray to the Lord.

THE LORD'S PRAYER
With these petitions in our hearts, we pray as the Lord taught us:
Our Father . . .

SHARING OF PEACE

CLOSING PRAYER
May the God of Love, who has loved us from our mother's womb, protect us tenderly throughout our lives and teach us the path of justice. We ask this in Christ's name. AMEN.

SATURDAY MORNING

✞

Lord, teach us justice.
And we shall live in your peace.

PSALM 7:3-11
℟ O God, in your mercy, call us back and convert our hearts.

O LORD my God, if I have done this,
    if there is wrong in my hands,
if I have repaid my ally with harm
    or plundered my foe without cause,
then let the enemy pursue and overtake me,
    trample my life to the ground,
    and lay my soul in the dust.

Rise up, O LORD, in your anger;
    lift yourself up against the fury of my enemies;
    awake, O my God; you have appointed a judgment.
Let the assembly of the peoples be gathered around you,
    and over it take your seat on high.
The LORD judges the peoples;
    judge me, O LORD, according to my righteousness
    and according to the integrity that is in me.

O let the evil of the wicked come to an end,
    but establish the righteous,
you who test the minds and hearts,
    O righteous God.

God is my shield,
> who saves the upright in heart.

God is a righteous judge,
> and a God who has indignation every day.

Glory to the Father . . .

SCRIPTURE   Joel 2:15-17, 26-27

Blow the trumpet in Zion;
> sanctify a fast;

call a solemn assembly;
> gather the people.

Sanctify the congregation;
> assemble the aged;

gather the children,
> even infants at the breast.

Let the bridegroom leave his room,
> and the bride her canopy.

Between the vestibule and the altar
> let the priests, the ministers of the LORD, weep.

Let them say, "Spare your people, O LORD,
> and do not make your heritage a mockery,
> a byword among the nations." . . .

[And the Lord responded:] You shall eat in plenty and be satisfied,
> and praise the name of the LORD your God,
> who has dealt wondrously with you.

And my people shall never again be put to shame.

You shall know that I am in the midst of Israel,
> and that I, the LORD, am your God and there is no other.

And my people shall never again be put to shame."

The Word of the Lord.

INTERCESSIONS
God-for-the-Poor, you have the power to lift up those who suffer, reprimand those who transgress, and restore justice throughout the earth. And so we pray: *Lord, teach us to live justly.*

- Grant all people, regardless of race, culture, gender, or social status, a just share in the bounty of the earth and full rights for self-determination. We pray to the Lord.
- Give policymakers in every nation and community the wisdom and courage to adopt laws and practices that benefit all people fairly. We pray to the Lord.
- Do not shame us, but call us back to love you in the faces of all we meet today. We pray to the Lord.
- For what else shall we pray this morning? [Pause for participants to add their own intentions.] We pray to the Lord.

THE LORD'S PRAYER
With these petitions in our hearts, we pray as the Lord taught us:
Our Father . . .

SHARING OF PEACE

CLOSING PRAYER
Ever-loving God, have mercy on our transgressions and teach us the way of justice for all women, children, and men throughout the world. We ask this in Christ's name. AMEN.

SATURDAY EVENING

Lord, teach us justice.
And we shall live in your peace.

PSALM 103:1-6, 13-14, 21-22
℟ O God, in your mercy, call us back and convert our hearts.

Bless the LORD, O my soul,
   and all that is within me,
    bless his holy name.
Bless the LORD, O my soul,
   and do not forget all his benefits—
who forgives all your iniquity,
   who heals all your diseases,
who redeems your life from the Pit,
   who crowns you with steadfast love and mercy,
who satisfies you with good as long as you live
   so that your youth is renewed like the eagle's.

The LORD works vindication
   and justice for all who are oppressed. . . .
As a father has compassion for his children,
   so the LORD has compassion for those who fear him.
For he knows how we were made;
   he remembers that we are dust. . . .
Bless the LORD, all his hosts,
   his ministers that do his will.

Bless the LORD, all his works,
    in all places of his dominion.
Bless the LORD, O my soul.

Glory to the Father . . .

SCRIPTURE   Mark 9:38-42, 49-50
John said to him, "Teacher, we saw someone casting out demons
in your name, and we tried to stop him, because he was not following us." But Jesus said, "Do not stop him; for no one who does
a deed of power in my name will be able soon afterward to speak
evil of me. Whoever is not against us is for us. For truly I tell you,
whoever gives you a cup of water to drink because you bear the
name of Christ will by no means lose the reward.

"If any of you put a stumbling block before one of these little
ones who believe in me, it would be better for you if a great
millstone were hung around your neck and you were thrown
into the sea. . . .

"For everyone will be salted with fire. Salt is good; but if salt has
lost its saltiness, how can you season it? Have salt in yourselves,
and be at peace with one another."

The Gospel of the Lord.

SILENT REFLECTION

INTERCESSIONS
God-for-the-Poor, you instructed us how to live justly through
your prophets and by the example of your Son, Jesus Christ. Give

us again your loving support as we strive to become your saving hands in the world. And so we pray: *Lord, teach us to live justly.*

- Lead us to be merciful, just, and fair in all that we do and say. We pray to the Lord.

- Renew our commitment to justice and instill our hearts with persistence and hope. We pray to the Lord.

- Grant those who have been denied money, opportunity, and respect greater access to these necessities, especially [pause for participants to add individual names or needs]. We pray to the Lord.

- For what else shall we pray because of our experiences today? [Pause for participants to add their own intentions.] We pray to the Lord.

THE LORD'S PRAYER
With these petitions in our hearts, we pray as the Lord taught us: Our Father . . .

SHARING OF PEACE

CLOSING PRAYER
Ever-loving God, let your justice prevail. Transform our world into a community of justice and peace according to your holy will. We ask this in Christ's name. AMEN.

Final Thoughts on the Challenge of Practicing Justice

The prayers for this week focus us on the work of transforming ourselves. This is the only possible way to create a more just society. The readings have urged us to practice justice; we experience how just practices transform our lives and the lives of other people.

This week, we can reflect on what we notice when we turn away from individualism, when the measure of goodness is the good of the least and the good of all. So we consider: What does it feel like for me when I place my desires and welfare alongside the needs of others? Whose needs are urgent and whose must be delayed or denied? In pondering God's steadfast love for us, how does it compare with the way we stand by those in need? What would happen if we really practiced justice?

Practicing justice will, over time, change our identity. Nevertheless, the short-term practicalities so often outweigh the patient reconstruction of our culture. Then we choose ease over persistent work. We need wisdom and experience to guide us. We also need hope.

Our hope is in God's promise that our work for justice will not be in vain. The promise of a new creation where God's order of justice will secure peace is ancient, striking a chord of longing deep in our hearts. After seeking forgiveness and reconciliation, after practicing justice, we turn our hearts in hope to the final week of the *Just Prayer* cycle. We turn to celebrate the assurance that every tear will be wiped away when God's justice is established on earth.

WEEK 4

JUSTICE CELEBRATED

CELEBRATING GOD'S JUSTICE AND THE PROMISE OF PEACE

This week places us in the "already, but not yet" truth of God's promise. Already justice is coming. It is present in our hearts. Justice names the "golden rule" that undergirds human society. Likewise, it is commanded in the sacred revelations of every faith tradition. We can recognize the slowly advancing values in the international community, which secure full rights for the powerless and vulnerable against the strong. Truly, justice dwells among us *already*.

Still, the fullness of God's justice is *not yet* here. We see sometimes that our efforts toward justice can yield a fragile peace or tentative gestures of goodwill. To keep us single-minded in the pursuit of justice, we are reminded: "If you desire peace, cultivate justice."* Our work continues to be planting the seeds of justice for a future harvest. This harvest, we hope, will be a world that is more just, more virtuous, and more peaceful than ours. Lasting peace remains a hope on the horizon, a light around the bend for the next generation.

---

* A translation of "Si vis pacem, cole justitiam," which is carved on the foundation of the International Labor Organization's original building in Geneva and was quoted by the Nobel Peace Prize committee awarding the ILO the prize in 1969 (http://www.nobelprize.org/nobel_prizes/peace/laureates/1969/labour-article.html). A similar phrase is attributed to Pope Paul VI: "If you want peace, work for justice."

While those seeds of justice are taking root, we can neverthe-less celebrate the new creation that God has promised. This final week in the cycle of *Just Prayer* rejoices in anticipation of a new beginning for creation. The morning Scripture readings, drawn principally from the great prophet Isaiah, describe the new Jeru-salem, the crowning glory of God's reign of justice. The four-week cycle ends with a final morning reading from the book of Reve-lation promising, "God himself will be with them; / he will wipe every tear from their eyes" (Rev 21:3-4). The gospel readings in the evenings draw upon Jesus' own description of the kingdom of heaven while also repeating his command that we ourselves are to establish the new creation with him, through our actions. The centerpiece of the readings is the "good Samaritan" story teaching us about universal compassion and justice. The interces-sions reflect the "already, but not yet" quality of the coming of justice. They continue to ask for transformation, greater justice among people now, and the remediation of specific injustices in the world. However, the tone shifts toward one of assurance, joy, and confidence in God's promise to make all things new.

This week of prayer closes on Saturday evening with the verse that closes the Christian Scriptures: *Maranatha!* "Come, Lord Jesus!" (Rev 22:20). With this plea, we emulate the first disciples who, after Jesus' ascension, praised God, practiced compassion, and waited for Christ's return with great joy. We can celebrate justice even now—already—because we trust God's promise.

SUNDAY MORNING

✝

Lord, teach us justice.
And we shall live in your peace.

PSALM 147:1-6, 10-11
℟ God's justice shall reach to the farthest seas; all humanity will
    share one peace.

Praise the LORD!
How good it is to sing praises to our God;
    for he is gracious, and a song of praise is fitting.
The LORD builds up Jerusalem;
    he gathers the outcasts of Israel.
He heals the brokenhearted,
    and binds up their wounds.
He determines the number of the stars;
    he gives to all of them their names.
Great is our Lord, and abundant in power;
    his understanding is beyond measure.
The LORD lifts up the downtrodden;
    he casts the wicked to the ground. . . .

His delight is not in the strength of the horse,
    nor his pleasure in the speed of a runner;

but the Lord takes pleasure in those who fear him,
   in those who hope in his steadfast love.

Glory to the Father . . .

SCRIPTURE   Isaiah 32:1-3, 16-18
See, a king will reign in righteousness,
   and princes will rule with justice.
Each will be like a hiding place from the wind,
   a covert from the tempest,
like streams of water in a dry place,
   like the shade of a great rock in a weary land.
Then the eyes of those who have sight will not be closed,
   and the ears of those who have hearing will listen. . . .

Then justice will dwell in the wilderness,
   and righteousness abide in the fruitful field.
The effect of righteousness will be peace,
   and the result of righteousness, quietness and trust forever.
My people will abide in a peaceful habitation,
   in secure dwellings, and in quiet resting places.

The Word of the Lord.

INTERCESSIONS
God of Possibilities, even now we glimpse a vision of a plentiful table where all are satisfied. It is not only your promise for our lives to come, but a reality that you command us to create here and now. And so we pray: *Lord, open our hearts to the poor among us.*

- Let your justice flow into every corner of our world so that those who have lived in need can flourish abundantly. We pray to the Lord.

- Encourage us to alleviate the suffering of those who lack basic needs right now as well as to strive for permanent solutions to global poverty. We pray to the Lord.

- Teach us to see you in the faces of those who depend upon our help. We pray to the Lord.

- For what else shall we pray this morning? [Pause for participants to add their own intentions.] We pray to the Lord.

THE LORD'S PRAYER
With these petitions in our hearts, we pray as the Lord taught us:
Our Father . . .

SHARING OF PEACE

CLOSING PRAYER
May the Lord of Justice send us unfailing courage to work for justice and hope for peace. We ask this in Christ's name. AMEN.

SUNDAY EVENING

✝

Lord, teach us justice.
And we shall live in your peace.

PSALM 145:3-10
℟ God's justice shall reach to the farthest seas; all humanity will
     share one peace.

Great is the LORD, and greatly to be praised;
     his greatness is unsearchable.

One generation shall laud your works to another,
     and shall declare your mighty acts.
On the glorious splendor of your majesty,
     and on your wondrous works, I will meditate.
The might of your awesome deeds shall be proclaimed,
     and I will declare your greatness.
They shall celebrate the fame of your abundant goodness,
     and shall sing aloud of your righteousness.
The LORD is gracious and merciful,
     slow to anger and abounding in steadfast love.
The LORD is good to all,
     and his compassion is over all that he has made.

All your works shall give thanks to you, O LORD,
     and all your faithful shall bless you.

Glory to the Father . . .

SCRIPTURE   Luke 12:22-25, 29-31

[Jesus] said to his disciples, "Therefore I tell you, do not worry about your life, what you will eat, or about your body, what you will wear. For life is more than food, and the body more than clothing. Consider the ravens: they neither sow nor reap, they have neither storehouse nor barn, and yet God feeds them. Of how much more value are you than the birds! And can any of you by worrying add a single hour to your span of life? . . . And do not keep striving for what you are to eat and what you are to drink, and do not keep worrying. For it is the nations of the world that strive after all these things, and your Father knows that you need them. Instead, strive for his kingdom, and these things will be given to you as well."

The Gospel of the Lord.

SILENT REFLECTION

INTERCESSIONS

Spirit of Possibilities, Jesus revealed your tender concern for all human needs and the possibility of a world governed in justice and peace. Inspire us to build the new Jerusalem, where there will be no more tears and no more need. And so we pray: *Lord, open our hearts to the poor among us.*

- Show us how to advocate for just laws and systems that permanently eliminate poverty. We pray to the Lord.
- Soften our hearts toward the needs of our neighbors, especially those who have no employment or income. We pray to the Lord.

- Come quickly to bring relief to the poor whose needs we have witnessed today, especially [pause for participants to add individual names or needs]. We pray to the Lord.
- For what else shall we pray because of our experiences today? [Pause for participants to add their own intentions.] We pray to the Lord.

THE LORD'S PRAYER
With these petitions in our hearts, we pray as the Lord taught us: Our Father . . .

SHARING OF PEACE

CLOSING PRAYER
May the God of Justice grant us courage and perseverance to work toward a future where all people on earth receive an abundant share of its riches. We ask this in Christ's name. AMEN.

MONDAY MORNING

✝

Lord, teach us justice.
And we shall live in your peace.

PSALM 98:1-4, 7-9
℟ God's justice shall reach to the farthest seas; all humanity will
    share one peace.

Sing to the LORD a new song,
    for he has done wondrous things.
His right hand and his holy arm
    have gotten him victory.
The LORD has made known his victory;
    he has revealed his vindication in the sight of the nations.
He has remembered his steadfast love and faithfulness
    to the house of Israel.
All the ends of the earth have seen
    the victory of our God.

Make a joyful noise to the LORD, all the earth;
    break forth into joyous song and sing praises. . . .

Let the sea roar, and all that fills it;
    the world and those who live in it.
Let the floods clap their hands;
    let the hills sing together for joy

at the presence of the Lord, for he is coming
>   to judge the earth.
He will judge the world with righteousness,
>   and the peoples with equity.

Glory to the Father . . .

SCRIPTURE   Isaiah 2:2-4
In days to come
>   the mountain of the Lord's house
shall be established as the highest of the mountains,
>   and shall be raised above the hills;
all the nations shall stream to it.
>   Many peoples shall come and say,
"Come, let us go up to the mountain of the Lord,
>   to the house of the God of Jacob;
that he may teach us his ways
>   and that we may walk in his paths."
For out of Zion shall go forth instruction,
>   and the word of the Lord from Jerusalem.
He shall judge between the nations,
>   and shall arbitrate for many peoples;
they shall beat their swords into plowshares,
>   and their spears into pruning hooks;
nation shall not lift up sword against nation,
>   neither shall they learn war any more.

The Word of the Lord.

INTERCESSIONS

Prince of Peace, we long for a time when weapons of war are never used and only tools for building peace remain. And so we pray: *Lord, may peace reign in our hearts and in our lives.*

- Give us courage to begin practicing nonviolence in our everyday lives. We pray to the Lord.

- Bring an end to violence that dehumanizes both victims and oppressors and usher in your reign of peace. We pray to the Lord.

- Shower your justice from east to west and from north to south, bringing all people together into one human community of peace. We pray to the Lord.

- For what else shall we pray this morning? [Pause for participants to add their own intentions.] We pray to the Lord.

THE LORD'S PRAYER

With these petitions in our hearts, we pray as the Lord taught us: Our Father . . .

SHARING OF PEACE

CLOSING PRAYER

May the God of Gentleness shelter us from harm and move us to pray unceasingly for justice and peace. We ask this in Christ's name. AMEN.

MONDAY EVENING

✝

Lord, teach us justice.
And we shall live in your peace.

PSALM 96:1-4, 7-8, 11-13
R̸ God's justice shall reach to the farthest seas; all humanity will
       share one peace.

O sing to the LORD a new song;
    sing to the LORD, all the earth.
Sing to the LORD, bless his name;
    tell of his salvation from day to day.
Declare his glory among the nations,
    his marvelous works among all the peoples.
For great is the LORD, and greatly to be praised;
    He is to be revered above all gods. . . .

Ascribe to the LORD, O families of the peoples,
    ascribe to the LORD glory and strength.
Ascribe to the LORD the glory due his name . . .

Let the heavens be glad, and let the earth rejoice;
    let the sea roar, and all that fills it . . .

Then shall all the trees of the forest sing for joy
    before the LORD; for he is coming,
    for he is coming to judge the earth.
He will judge the world with righteousness,
    and the peoples with his truth.

Glory to the Father . . .

SCRIPTURE   Luke 18:15-17

People were bringing even infants to [Jesus] that he might touch them; and when the disciples saw it, they sternly ordered them not to do it. But Jesus called for them and said, "Let the little children come to me, and do not stop them; for it is to such as these that the kingdom of God belongs. Truly I tell you, whoever does not receive the kingdom of God as a little child will never enter it."

The Word of the Lord.

SILENT REFLECTION

INTERCESSIONS

Spirit of Peace, we have strayed from the serenity of your kingdom. Renew our hearts to desire peace completely. And so we pray: *Lord, may peace reign in our hearts and in our lives.*

- Keep us from hurting each other and help us create a world where children, women, and men can live securely. We pray to the Lord.

- Plant peace in our heart and show us the way to live without violence. We pray to the Lord.

- Wipe away the sufferings of your people, especially [pause for participants to add individual names or needs]. We pray to the Lord.

- For what else shall we pray because of our experiences today? [Pause for participants to add their own intentions.] We pray to the Lord.

THE LORD'S PRAYER
With these petitions in our hearts, we pray as the Lord taught us:
Our Father . . .

SHARING OF PEACE

CLOSING PRAYER
May the God of Gentleness humble our hearts and teach us to be
at peace with people of all nations, faiths, and cultures. We ask
this in Christ's name. AMEN.

TUESDAY MORNING

✝

Lord, teach us justice.
And we shall live in your peace.

PSALM 101:1-6
℟ God's justice shall reach to the farthest seas; all humanity will
       share one peace.

I will sing of loyalty and of justice;
    to you, O LORD, I will sing.
I will study the way that is blameless.
    When shall I attain it?

I will walk with integrity of heart
    within my house;
I will not set before my eyes
    anything that is base.

I hate the work of those who fall away;
    it shall not cling to me.
Perverseness of heart shall be far from me;
    I will know nothing of evil.
One who secretly slanders a neighbor
    I will destroy.
A haughty look and an arrogant heart
    I will not tolerate.

I will look with favor on the faithful in the land,
    so that they may live with me;
whoever walks in the way that is blameless
    shall minister to me.

Glory to the Father . . .

SCRIPTURE   Isaiah 26:1-7
On that day this song will be sung in the land of Judah:
We have a strong city;
    he sets up victory
    like walls and bulwarks.
Open the gates,
    so that the righteous nation that keeps faith
    may enter in.
Those of steadfast mind you keep in peace—
    in peace because they trust in you.
Trust in the LORD forever,
    for in the LORD GOD
    you have an everlasting rock.
For he has brought low
    the inhabitants of the height;
    the lofty city he lays low.
He lays it low to the ground,
    casts it to the dust.
The foot tramples it,
    the feet of the poor,
    the steps of the needy.

The way of the righteous is level;
    O Just One, you make smooth the path of the righteous.

The Word of the Lord.

INTERCESSIONS

God of all nations and peoples, you promise a new earth, where all are fully known and welcome. In ways large and small, move us to welcome into our communities immigrants, travelers, and those seeking asylum. And so we pray: *Lord, teach us to welcome each person who comes to us in need.*

- Protect people who have fled their homes and bring them to safety. We pray to the Lord.

- Unite your people to build a future where the dignity of all human beings is respected, regardless of their nationality, documentation, or citizenship. We pray to the Lord.

- Rouse our leaders to pass immigration laws that support the free movement of people around the globe. We pray to the Lord.

- For what else shall we pray this morning? [Pause for participants to add their own intentions.] We pray to the Lord.

THE LORD'S PRAYER

With these petitions in our hearts, we pray as the Lord taught us: Our Father . . .

SHARING OF PEACE

CLOSING PRAYER

May the God of Welcome inspire us with a vision of the new Jerusalem as we build a city where all are welcome here and now. We ask this in Christ's name. AMEN.

TUESDAY EVENING

✝

Lord, teach us justice.
And we shall live in your peace.

PSALM 146
℟ God's justice shall reach to the farthest seas; all humanity will
    share one peace.

Praise the Lord!
Praise the Lord, O my soul!
I will praise the Lord as long as I live;
    I will sing praises to my God all my life long.

Do not put your trust in princes,
    in mortals, in whom there is no help.
When their breath departs, they return to the earth;
    on that very day their plans perish.

Happy are those whose help is the God of Jacob,
    whose hope is in the Lord their God,
who made heaven and earth,
    the sea, and all that is in them;
who keeps faith forever;
    who executes justice for the oppressed;
    who gives food to the hungry.

The Lord sets the prisoners free;
    the Lord opens the eyes of the blind.
The Lord lifts up those who are bowed down;
    the Lord loves the righteous.

The LORD watches over the strangers;
   he upholds the orphan and the widow,
   but the way of the wicked he brings to ruin.
The LORD will reign forever,
   your God, O Zion, for all generations.
Praise the LORD!

Glory to the Father . . .

SCRIPTURE   Matthew 13:31-33, 44-46
[Jesus] put before them another parable: "The kingdom of heaven
is like a mustard seed that someone took and sowed in his field;
it is the smallest of all the seeds, but when it has grown it is the
greatest of shrubs and becomes a tree, so that the birds of the air
come and make nests in its branches."

He told them another parable: "The kingdom of heaven is like
yeast that a woman took and mixed in with three measures of
flour until all of it was leavened." . . .

[He also said,] "The kingdom of heaven is like treasure hidden
in a field, which someone found and hid; then in his joy he goes
and sells all that he has and buys that field.

"Again, the kingdom of heaven is like a merchant in search of
fine pearls; on finding one pearl of great value, he went and sold
all that he had and bought it."

The Gospel of the Lord.

SILENT REFLECTION

INTERCESSIONS

God of all nations and people, you desire for every human being to live in peace and safety. Make us single-minded in our commitment to a just community. And so we pray: *Lord, teach us to welcome each person who comes to us in need.*

- Protect women and men who have left their homes this year due to economic upheaval or insecurity and help them find meaningful work. We pray to the Lord.

- Encourage employers who rely on displaced and migrant workers to pay them fairly and treat them with dignity. We pray to the Lord.

- Bless those who must travel to find a better life, especially [pause for participants to add individual names or needs]. We pray to the Lord.

- For what else shall we pray because of our experiences today? [Pause for participants to add their own intentions.] We pray to the Lord.

THE LORD'S PRAYER

With these petitions in our hearts, we pray as the Lord taught us: Our Father . . .

SHARING OF PEACE

CLOSING PRAYER

May the God of Welcome instill in us the gift of hospitality to protect strangers, shelter travelers, and give sanctuary to refugees; and may our hospitality yield the fruits of justice and peace. We ask this in Christ's name. AMEN.

WEDNESDAY MORNING

✝

Lord, teach us justice.
And we shall live in your peace.

PSALM 138:1-5
℟ God's justice shall reach to the farthest seas; all humanity will
    share one peace.

I give you thanks, O LORD, with my whole heart;
    before the gods I sing your praise;
I bow down toward your holy temple
    and give thanks to your name for your steadfast love and your
        faithfulness;
    for you have exalted your name and your word
    above everything.
On the day I called, you answered me,
    you increased my strength of soul.

All the kings of the earth shall praise you, O LORD,
    for they have heard the words of your mouth.
They shall sing of the ways of the LORD,
    for great is the glory of the LORD.

Glory to the Father . . .

SCRIPTURE   Genesis 2:8-9, 15

And the Lord God planted a garden in Eden, in the east; and there he put the man whom he had formed. Out of the ground the Lord God made to grow every tree that is pleasant to the sight and good for food, the tree of life also in the midst of the garden, and the tree of the knowledge of good and evil. . . .

The Lord God took the man and put him in the garden of Eden to till it and keep it.

The Word of the Lord.

INTERCESSIONS

God of Life, until your justice prevails in creation, we ask for wisdom to care for your world and share its blessings with all people. And so we pray: *Wellspring of Life, make us wise stewards of the earth and its blessings.*

- Inspire us to conserve resources and live simply. We pray to the Lord.
- Move us to advocate for effective environmental policies that assure everyone will have access to clean water, pure air, and healthy food. We pray to the Lord.
- Inspire us to praise you unceasingly for the goodness and beauty in our lives. We pray to the Lord.
- For what else shall we pray this morning? [Pause for participants to add their own intentions.] We pray to the Lord.

THE LORD'S PRAYER
With these petitions in our hearts, we pray as the Lord taught us:
Our Father . . .

SHARING OF PEACE

CLOSING PRAYER
May the God of Creation give us the wisdom and skill to protect
our planet's health so that its bounty will support life of every
kind. We ask this in Christ's name. AMEN.

WEDNESDAY EVENING

✝

Lord, teach us justice.
And we shall live in your peace.

PSALM 72:2, 4-7, 17-19
℟ God's justice shall reach to the farthest seas; all humanity will
      share one peace.

May [the Holy One] judge your people with righteousness,
    and your poor with justice. . . .
May he defend the cause of the poor of the people,
    give deliverance to the needy,
    and crush the oppressor.

May he live while the sun endures,
    and as long as the moon, throughout all generations.
May he be like rain that falls on the mown grass,
    like showers that water the earth.
In his days may righteousness flourish
    and peace abound, until the moon is no more. . . .

May his name endure forever,
    his fame continue as long as the sun. . . .

Blessed be the LORD, the God of Israel,
    who alone does wondrous things.
Blessed be his glorious name forever;
    may his glory fill the whole earth.
Amen and Amen.

Glory to the Father . . .

SCRIPTURE   Luke 24:13-17, 27-32

Now on that same day two of them were going to a village called Emmaus, about seven miles from Jerusalem, and talking with each other about all these things that had happened. While they were talking and discussing, Jesus himself came near and went with them, but their eyes were kept from recognizing him. And he said to them, "What are you discussing with each other while you walk along?" They stood still, looking sad. . . . Then beginning with Moses and all the prophets, he interpreted to them the things about himself in all the Scriptures.

As they came near the village to which they were going, he walked ahead as if he were going on. But they urged him strongly, saying, "Stay with us, because it is almost evening and the day is now nearly over." So he went in to stay with them. When he was at the table with them, he took bread, blessed and broke it, and gave it to them. Then their eyes were opened, and they recognized him; and he vanished from their sight. They said to each other, "Were not our hearts burning within us while he was talking to us on the road, while he was opening the scriptures to us?"

The Gospel of the Lord.

SILENT REFLECTION

INTERCESSIONS

Breath of Life, we know your tender love for us through your Word and your world. We can taste and see your good creation. And so we pray: *Wellspring of Life, make us wise stewards of the earth and its blessings.*

- Inspire people to give you thanks for productive soil, abundant rain, and sunshine in due season. We pray to the Lord.
- Teach us to live gently upon the earth and to instruct our children to respect this planet that all people share. We pray to the Lord.
- For those who are excluded from the earth's riches and beauty, especially [pause for participants to add individual names or needs]. We pray to the Lord.
- For what else shall we pray because of our experiences today? [Pause for participants to add their own intentions.] We pray to the Lord.

THE LORD'S PRAYER
With these petitions in our hearts, we pray as the Lord taught us:
Our Father . . .

SHARING OF PEACE

CLOSING PRAYER
May the God of Creation, who gives us life, bless and preserve life on the earth until all people live together in the new creation of justice and peace. We ask this in Christ's name. AMEN.

THURSDAY MORNING

✝

Lord, teach us justice.
And we shall live in your peace.

PSALM 33:3-5, 8, 11-12, 20-22
℟ God's justice shall reach to the farthest seas; all humanity will
    share one peace.

Sing to [the Lord] a new song;
    play skillfully on the strings, with loud shouts.

For the word of the LORD is upright,
    and all his work is done in faithfulness.
He loves righteousness and justice;
    the earth is full of the steadfast love of the LORD. . . .

Let all the earth fear the LORD;
    let all the inhabitants of the world stand in awe of him. . . .

The counsel of the LORD stands forever,
    the thoughts of his heart to all generations.
Happy is the nation whose God is the LORD,
    the people whom he has chosen as his heritage. . . .
Our soul waits for the LORD;
    he is our help and shield.

Our heart is glad in him,
    because we trust in his holy name.
Let your steadfast love, O LORD, be upon us,
    even as we hope in you.

Glory to the Father . . .

SCRIPTURE   Isaiah 11:1-5
A shoot shall come out from the stump of Jesse,
    and a branch shall grow out of his roots.
The spirit of the LORD shall rest on him,
    the spirit of wisdom and understanding,
    the spirit of counsel and might,
    the spirit of knowledge and the fear of the LORD.
His delight shall be in the fear of the LORD.

He shall not judge by what his eyes see,
    or decide by what his ears hear;
but with righteousness he shall judge the poor,
    and decide with equity for the meek of the earth;
he shall strike the earth with the rod of his mouth,
    and with the breath of his lips he shall kill the wicked.
Righteousness shall be the belt around his waist,
    and faithfulness the belt around his loins.

The Word of the Lord.

INTERCESSIONS
Healing God, you offer your people hope for a time when sickness and sorrow will be wiped away. And so, in anticipation of that time of joy, we pray: *Just Lord, heal our troubled world and grant us peace.*

- Bless the sick; grant them health now and usher them into your kingdom at their life's end. We pray to the Lord.

- Heal us in mind, body, and spirit. We pray to the Lord.

- Safeguard those who turn to you for healing today. We pray to the Lord.

- For what else shall we pray this morning? [Pause for participants to add their own intentions.] We pray to the Lord.

THE LORD'S PRAYER

With these petitions in our hearts, we pray as the Lord taught us: Our Father . . .

SHARING OF PEACE

CLOSING PRAYER

May God the Source of Life send peace into our hearts so that all people can live together with dignity, hope, and health. We ask this in Christ's name. AMEN.

THURSDAY EVENING

✝

Lord, teach us justice.
And we shall live in your peace.

PSALM 46:1-3, 7-10
R̸ God's justice shall reach to the farthest seas; all humanity will
        share one peace.

God is our refuge and strength,
    a very present help in trouble.
Therefore we will not fear, though the earth should change,
    though the mountains shake in the heart of the sea;
though its waters roar and foam,
    though the mountains tremble with its tumult. . . .

The LORD of hosts is with us;
    the God of Jacob is our refuge.
Come, behold the works of the LORD . . .
He makes wars cease to the end of the earth;
    he breaks the bow, and shatters the spear;
    he burns the shields with fire.
"Be still, and know that I am God!
    I am exalted among the nations,
    I am exalted in the earth."

Glory to the Father . . .

SCRIPTURE   Mark 1:1-4, 9-11

The beginning of the good news of Jesus Christ, the Son of God. As it is written in the prophet Isaiah,

> "See, I am sending my messenger ahead of you,
>> who will prepare your way;
> the voice of one crying out in the wilderness;
>> 'Prepare the way of the Lord,
>> make his paths straight,'"

John the Baptist appeared in the wilderness, proclaiming a baptism of repentance for the forgiveness of sins. . . .

In those days Jesus came from Nazareth of Galilee and was baptized by John in the Jordan. And just as he was coming up out of the water, he saw the heavens torn apart and the Spirit descending like a dove on him. And a voice came from heaven, "You are my Son, the Beloved; with you I am well pleased."

The Gospel of the Lord.

SILENT REFLECTION

INTERCESSIONS

Healing Spirit, Jesus showed us how to heal the sick in compassion and gentleness. We need your Holy Spirit, now, to inspire us to follow Christ's example faithfully. And so we pray: *Just Lord, heal our troubled world and grant us peace.*

- Give insight to researchers seeking cures for diseases plaguing humanity and rouse benefactors and governments to fund their efforts generously. We pray to the Lord.

- Guide our leaders to make health care available to all residents of our nation. We pray to the Lord.
- Fill us with tender compassion for all who suffer from illness and affliction, especially for [pause for participants to add individual names or needs]. We pray to the Lord.
- For what else shall we pray because of our experiences today? [Pause for participants to add their own intentions.] We pray to the Lord.

THE LORD'S PRAYER
With these petitions in our hearts, we pray as the Lord taught us:
Our Father . . .

SHARING OF PEACE

CLOSING PRAYER
May God the Source of Life inspire us to work earnestly to eliminate diseases and hardships caused by poverty and injustice. We ask this in Christ's name. AMEN.

FRIDAY MORNING

✝

Lord, teach us justice.
And we shall live in your peace.

PSALM 19:1-4, 7-10
℞ God's justice shall reach to the farthest seas; all humanity will
        share one peace.

The heavens are telling the glory of God;
    and the firmament proclaims his handiwork.
Day to day pours forth speech,
    and night to night declares knowledge.
There is no speech, nor are there words;
    their voice is not heard;
yet their voice goes out through all the earth,
    and their words to the end of the world. . . .

The law of the LORD is perfect,
    reviving the soul;
the decrees of the LORD are sure,
    making wise the simple;
the precepts of the LORD are right,
    rejoicing the heart;
the commandment of the LORD is clear,
    enlightening the eyes;
the fear of the LORD is pure,
    enduring forever;

the ordinances of the Lord are true
  and righteous altogether.
More to be desired are they than gold,
  even much fine gold;
sweeter also than honey,
  and drippings of the honeycomb.

Glory to the Father . . .

SCRIPTURE   Isaiah 61:1-3, 8-9
The spirit of the Lord God is upon me,
  because the Lord has anointed me;
he has sent me to bring good news to the oppressed,
  to bind up the brokenhearted,
to proclaim liberty to the captives,
  and release to the prisoners;
to proclaim the year of the Lord's favor,
  and the day of vengeance of our God;
  to comfort all who mourn;
to provide for those who mourn in Zion—
  to give them a garland instead of ashes,
the oil of gladness instead of mourning,
  the mantle of praise instead of a faint spirit. . . .
  I will make an everlasting covenant with them.
Their descendants shall be known among the nations,
  and their offspring among the peoples;
all who see them shall acknowledge
  that they are a people whom the Lord has blessed.

The Word of the Lord.

INTERCESSIONS

God of Comfort, you bind the wounds of people who are injured; you comfort those in mourning; and you offer the joy of your presence to all human beings. And so, relying on your eternal promise of salvation, we pray: *Show us your mercy, O Lord.*

- Remove all barriers that exclude women from full participation in social, political, and economic life. We pray to the Lord.
- Comfort widows and orphans, and all people who have lost loved ones on whom they depended; bring them hope for a new future according to your promise. We pray to the Lord.
- Rouse governments to provide equal education, training, and economic opportunities for women and girls. We pray to the Lord.
- For what else shall we pray this morning? [Pause for participants to add their own intentions.] We pray to the Lord.

THE LORD'S PRAYER

With these petitions in our hearts, we pray as the Lord taught us: Our Father . . .

SHARING OF PEACE

CLOSING PRAYER

May the God of Solace use our hands and hearts to bring justice and peace into every land and nation. We ask this in Christ's name. AMEN.

FRIDAY EVENING

✝

Lord, teach us justice.
And we shall live in your peace.

PSALM 48:1-3, 12-14
℟ God's justice shall reach to the farthest seas; all humanity will
            share one peace.

Great is the LORD and greatly to be praised
      in the city of our God.
His holy mountain, beautiful in elevation,
      is the joy of all the earth,
Mount Zion, in the far north,
      the city of the great King.
Within its citadels God
      has shown himself a sure defense. . . .

Walk about Zion, go all around it,
      count its towers,
consider well its ramparts;
      go through its citadels,
that you may tell the next generation
      that this is God,
our God forever and ever.

Glory to the Father . . .

SCRIPTURE   Luke 10:30-37

Jesus [told this story:] "A man was going down from Jerusalem to Jericho, and fell into the hands of robbers, who stripped him, beat him, and went away, leaving him half dead. Now by chance a priest was going down that road; and when he saw him, he passed by on the other side. So likewise a Levite, when he came to the place and saw him, passed by on the other side. But a Samaritan while traveling came near him; and when he saw him, he was moved with pity. He went to him and bandaged his wounds, having poured oil and wine on them. Then he put him on his own animal, brought him to an inn, and took care of him. The next day he took out two denarii, gave them to the innkeeper, and said, 'Take care of him; and when I come back, I will repay you whatever more you spend.' Which of these three, do you think, was a neighbor to the man who fell into the hands of the robbers?" [The young man] said, "The one who showed him mercy." Jesus said to him, "Go and do likewise."

The Gospel of the Lord.

SILENT REFLECTION

INTERCESSIONS

Spirit of Comfort, we celebrate your goodness to us and we ask for your strength to care for all people as neighbors, as Jesus taught us. And so we pray: *Show us your mercy, O Lord.*

- Open our hearts to recognize people of all genders, races, religions, and cultures as neighbors who deserve our respect and care. We pray to the Lord.

- Comfort and provide special blessings for women and girls, mothers and children, widows and wives. We pray to the Lord.

- Safeguard all your people who urgently need special protection from injustice and discrimination, especially [pause for participants to add individual names or needs]. We pray to the Lord.

- For what else shall we pray because of our experiences today? [Pause for participants to add their own intentions.] We pray to the Lord.

THE LORD'S PRAYER

With these petitions in our hearts, we pray as the Lord taught us: Our Father . . .

SHARING OF PEACE

CLOSING PRAYER

May the God of Solace give us courage to seek justice for all people as we wait in hope for the advent of justice and peace. We ask this in Christ's name. AMEN.

SATURDAY MORNING

✝

Lord, teach us justice.
And we shall live in your peace.

PSALM 122
℟ God's justice shall reach to the farthest seas; all humanity will
    share one peace.

I was glad when they said to me,
    "Let us go to the house of the LORD!"
Our feet are standing
    within your gates, O Jerusalem.

Jerusalem—built as a city
    that is bound firmly together.
To it the tribes go up,
    the tribes of the LORD,
as was decreed for Israel,
    to give thanks to the name of the LORD.
For there the thrones for judgment were set up,
    the thrones of the house of David.

Pray for the peace of Jerusalem:
    "May they prosper who love you.
Peace be within your walls,
    and security within your towers."

For the sake of my relatives and friends
    I will say, "Peace be within you."
For the sake of the house of the LORD our God,
    I will seek your good.

Glory to the Father . . .

SCRIPTURE   Rev 21:1-5
Then I saw a new heaven and a new earth; for the first heaven
and the first earth had passed away, and the sea was no more.
And I saw the holy city, the new Jerusalem, coming down out of
heaven from God, prepared as a bride adorned for her husband.
And I heard a loud voice from the throne saying,

"See, the home of God is among [human beings].
He will dwell with them;
they will be his peoples,
and God himself will be with them;
he will wipe every tear from their eyes.
Death will be no more;
mourning and crying and pain will be no more,
for the first things have passed away."

And the one who was seated on the throne said, "See, I am
making all things new."

The Word of the Lord.

INTERCESSIONS

God of Joy, trusting your steadfast love, we yearn for a world where no one suffers from discrimination, exclusion, or injustice. As we wait for this new earth, we pray: *Lord, teach us to live justly.*

- Assist nations to formulate policies and laws that promote a more equal distribution of wealth and that repair past injustices. We pray to the Lord.

- Teach us to stand in solidarity with neighbors of diverse races, religions, backgrounds, and cultures as we work for inclusive and just institutions. We pray to the Lord.

- Do not delay in sending your justice upon the earth. We pray to the Lord.

- For what else shall we pray this morning? [Pause for participants to add their own intentions.] We pray to the Lord.

THE LORD'S PRAYER

With these petitions in our hearts, we pray as the Lord taught us: Our Father . . .

SHARING OF PEACE

CLOSING PRAYER

May the God of Justice and Peace give us open hearts and understanding minds to appreciate diversity and cultivate respect, dignity, and justice for all people. We ask this in Christ's name. AMEN.

SATURDAY EVENING

✝

Lord, teach us justice.
And we shall live in your peace.

PSALM 112:1-7, 9
℟ God's justice shall reach to the farthest seas; all humanity will
        share one peace.

Praise the LORD!
    Happy are those who fear the LORD,
    who greatly delight in his commandments.
Their descendants will be mighty in the land;
    the generation of the upright will be blessed.
Wealth and riches are in their houses,
    and their righteousness endures forever.
They rise in the darkness as a light for the upright;
    they are gracious, merciful, and righteous.
It is well with those who deal generously and lend,
    who conduct their affairs with justice.
For the righteous will never be moved;
    they will be remembered forever.
They are not afraid of evil tidings;
    their hearts are firm, secure in the LORD. . . .
They have distributed freely, they have given to the poor;
    their righteousness endures forever;
    their horn is exalted in honor.

Glory to the Father . . .

SCRIPTURE   John 13:4-8, 12-15

[Jesus] got up from the table, took off his outer robe, and tied a towel around himself. Then he poured water into a basin and began to wash the disciples' feet and to wipe them with the towel that was tied around him. He came to Simon Peter, who said to him, "Lord, are you going to wash my feet?" Jesus answered, "You do not know now what I am doing, but later you will understand." Peter said to him, "You will never wash my feet." Jesus answered, "Unless I wash you, you have no share with me." . . .

After he had washed their feet, had put on his robe, and had returned to the table, he said to them, "Do you know what I have done to you? You call me Teacher and Lord—and you are right, for that is what I am. So if I, your Lord and Teacher, have washed your feet, you also ought to wash one another's feet. For I have set you an example, that you also should do as I have done to you.

The Gospel of the Lord.

SILENT REFLECTION

INTERCESSIONS

Spirit of Joy, by Christ's example, we know how to serve each other to bring about an order of peace. Still, we need your grace to follow him, and so we pray: *Lord, teach us to live justly.*

- Impart to us a willingness to conduct all our affairs, public and private, small and large, with justice and equity. We pray to the Lord.

- Inspire our leaders with a true desire to eliminate disparities of health, wealth, power, and influence among people so that everyone may share fully in the earth's gifts. We pray to the Lord.

- For all who are excluded from human society and its benefits, especially [pause for participants to add individual names or needs]. We pray to the Lord.

- For what else shall we pray because of our experiences today? [Pause for participants to add their own intentions.] We pray to the Lord.

THE LORD'S PRAYER
With these petitions in our hearts, we pray as the Lord taught us: Our Father . . .

SHARING OF PEACE

CLOSING PRAYER
May the God of Justice and Peace come quickly to create the world anew. Maranatha! Come, Lord Jesus! AMEN.

Final Thoughts on the Reign of God's Justice

We have come full circle. God's command to live justly will bear fruit as the peace of the new creation. Still, in this fourth week of the *Just Prayer* cycle, our actions and prayers remain in tension. We work for justice as God commands, yet we celebrate in anticipation the peace God has promised will come.

Working for justice means more than specific practices. It means allowing ourselves to be transformed by grace into more just people. The readings from this week offer so much richness for meditation. We can reflect first upon our own transformation: Where do I place my trust? Is my frame of reference my own good or can I claim that I love my neighbor as myself? We also need to consider the process of growth and change: What keeps me from choosing a just outcome? Is it fear, a lack of understanding, or a loss of hope? When we understand what holds us back, then we can bring it in prayer to God and seek conversion.

To celebrate justice now is to celebrate our own small victories. As the book of Daniel reminds us, those who lead many to justice shall be "like the stars forever" (12:3). When we commit to justice, we commit ourselves to the daily task of creating and shaping a more just and peaceful community. This future is not only for ourselves, but also for our sisters and brothers, for the generations to come. Justice is God's command; it is our joyful hope. In this world of "already, but not yet" justice, our hope lives as confidence in God's tender love for us and the joy of God's kingdom to come.

CHOOSING JUSTICE

Choosing justice means changing our frame of reference, changing our very selves. Unfortunately, campaigns and strategies to improve human behavior are as old as the Ten Commandments, perhaps as ancient as humanity itself, and often unsuccessful. "Do this, avoid that." The efforts of preachers, psychologists, healers, and parents have rarely moved us to become better people. We can almost hear the exasperation in the prophet Micah's rhetorical challenge: "What does the Lord require of you / but to do justice, and to love kindness, / and to walk humbly with your God?" (6:8). So how are we to think about choosing and changing so that God's justice can dwell more fully in our world? After we have prayed and practiced justice over days and weeks, here are some considerations for reflection.

First, we can begin with freedom. The hallmark of our humanity is the freedom God has given us. Our lives are poised at the crossroad of the present moment, when we are fully conscious of the past choices and future opportunities. In our freedom, God offers us the responsibility to create ourselves and the world around us by the choices we make. We are invited to join God in creating a just and peaceful world. God gives us the freedom to accept the invitation. The Holy Spirit instills in us the desire for justice. And Jesus shows us how to be just people by his example. To choose justice is to choose to join the Holy Trinity in the creation and recreation of the world. In this present moment and in every moment, we can claim the gift of divine freedom.

Second, we can examine our personal identity. Our identity is the context for our actions. Our frame of reference in turn dictates the circle of our concern. When our identity is framed in terms of family, race, religion, or social class, the interests of the group circumscribe our interests. Fortunately, we can redefine our identity and the Christian Scriptures offer us two excellent examples. Through the parable of the Good Samaritan, Jesus charged his listeners to expand their definition of neighbor. Essentially, he challenged them to expand their own identity to include even enemies. Even more compelling is God's own changed identity, through the incarnation. Saint Paul's great hymn proclaims that the Word of God emptied himself to take on our humanity: Christ did not cling to his divinity, but claimed our humanity as his own, with all its flaws and miseries, to love us and dwell with us (Phil 2:6-7). We might label the incarnation an act of divine solidarity, according to Catholic social teaching, because God stands with humanity, taking on our burdens as God's own. If we want to mature in our love for others, we must release our own concerns in trust to God, and take on the concerns of others as ours. In this way, we begin to act for the good of the community, for the good of the whole, which is justice.

Third, we can practice justice. Practicing justice, however, cannot be naïve, ill-informed, or an exercise of charity through privilege. We need to immerse ourselves in life so that the contrast between justice and injustice is stark and palpable. Through direct experience, we develop a more immediate understanding of what is at stake. We can test our presuppositions against the lives of our community, integrating the experiences of all into a more informed and authentic perspective. Finally, according to the old adage, practice makes perfect. We become people who make just decisions when we practice justice until it becomes second nature.

Finally, there is prayer. Our ingrained habits and our cultural context shape our values so decidedly that the boundaries of our lives are often invisible to us. These boundaries are as stubborn and tenacious as our personal sins. Such demons are so powerful that they can only be cast out through prayer, as Jesus told his disciples. Really, this is the very nature of sin—sin *is* sin because it cannot be eradicated without God's help. Christ's incarnation is evidence that we cannot simply make ourselves better people. Human beings need the grace of God to be saved. In prayer, we present ourselves humbly before God seeking grace to become just people. So, in some profound and essential way, there is just prayer. Maranatha!

SELECTED BIBLIOGRAPHY

Prayer and Outreach

These resources for prayer and outreach were selected for their sensitivity and comprehensiveness and, in some cases, for the background context they offer on particular issues. The selections offer additional ideas to expand our awareness and responses to problems of injustice in the world today. Groups who are regularly involved with justice and service are encouraged to create their own resource repository and share it with others.

General Resources

Catholic Relief Services. http://education.crs.org/prayers/.

Center of Concern: Education for Justice. https://educationforjustice.org.

Inclusive Language Liturgy of the Hours. http://www.rci.rutgers.edu/~lcrew/joyanyway/joy25.html.

United Nations. Millennium Development Goals. http://www.un.org/millenniumgoals/poverty.shtml.

United States Conference of Catholic Bishops. Everyday Christianity: To Hunger and Thirst for Justice. http://www.usccb.org/beliefs-and-teachings/what-we-believe/catholic-social-teaching/everyday-christianity-to-hunger-and-thirst-for-justice.cfm.

———. Justice, Peace, and Human Development. http://www.usccb.org/about/justice-peace-and-human-development/.

On Global Solidarity among All People

Catholic Diocese of Cincinnati. http://www.catholiccincinnati.org/wp-content/uploads/2011/01/intercession.pdf.

United States Conference of Catholic Bishops. Called to Global Solidarity. http://www.usccb.org/issues-and-action/human-life-and-dignity/global-issues/called-to-global-solidarity-international-challenges-for-u-s-parishes.cfm.

On Poverty

Catholics Confront Global Poverty. http://www.confrontglobalpoverty
.org/our-faith-global-poverty/prayer-spirituality/.

The Sanctuary Centre. http://www.thesanctuarycentre.org/resources
/written-prayers-intercessions-responding-to-global-poverty-issues
.pdf.

On War and Violence

Overcoming Violence: Churches Seeking Reconciliation and Peace.
http://overcomingviolence.org/en/decade-to-overcome-violence
/about-dov/international-day-of-prayer-for/resources/prayers-2005
.html.

On Immigration and Refugees

Diocese of Camden. http://camdenlifejustice.files.wordpress.com/2013
/03/immigration-packet-for-parishes.pdf.

Minnesota Catholic Conference. http://www.mncc.org/wp-content
/uploads/2012/11/Immigration-Sunday-Resource-and-Liturgy
-Planning-Guide-2013.pdf.

On Climate and Environmental Concerns

Caritas Australia. http://www.caritas.org.au/docs/campaigns/a-just
-climate-prayers-of-intercession.pdf?sfvrsn=6.

Spring Hill College. Environmental Justice Library. http://www.shc.edu
/theolibrary/environ.htm.

On Health and Human Well-Being

Church and Friary of Saint Francis of Assisi. http://www.stfrancisnyc
.org/devotions/prayers-for-the-sick/.

Out of the Depths (mental illness). http://nouwennetwork1234
.wordpress.com/2013/11/24/prayers-for-refugees-and-asylum
-seekers/.

On the Well-Being of Women and Children

World Vision. http://www.worldvision.org/news/july-prayer-focus
-pray-women-and-girls.

Yale Divinity School. http://www.yale.edu/divinity/fb/3rdSundayprayers
.pdf.

Additional Resources

Some of these additional resources provide biblical and theological foundations to contextualize the basic notion of justice or an individual theme within the larger idea of justice. Other resources inspire and engage us in the struggle for justice for the people of our world.

Ahern, Kevin, ed. *The Radical Bible*. Maryknoll, NY: Orbis, 2009. Practical, pocket-sized selection of interfaith readings, quotes, and teachings on social justice.

Allaire, James, and Rosemary Broughton. *Praying with Dorothy Day*. Winona, MN: St. Mary's Press, 1995. A meditation guide drawing upon the spirituality and writings of Dorothy Day, cofounder of the Catholic Worker Movement.

Bible Odyssey. http://www.bibleodyssey.org/. Academic study of the Bible with contributions from scholars across the United States. Sample essays include: Brettler, Marc Zvi, "The Prophets and the Temple"; Houston, Walter J., "Social Justice and the Prophets"; Landau, Brent, "The Benedictus"; Powell, Mark Allan, "The Beatitudes"; Tannehill, Robert C., "The Magnificat"; Weaver, Dorothy Jean, "Concepts of the Sermon on the Mount."

Cloutier, David. *Walking God's Earth: The Environment and Catholic Faith*. Collegeville, MN: Liturgical Press, 2014. Explores the significance and implications of the environment in the Catholic tradition.

Friend, Shelby M. *Trouble Don't Last Always*. Bloomington, IN: Author House, 2008. Roman Catholic deacon and African American, Friend's memoir of struggle and persistence from roots in poverty in rural Tennessee.

Guzder, Deena. *Divine Rebels: American Christian Activists for Social Justice*. Chicago: Lawrence Hill Books, 2011. Profiles of American Christian activists since the 1950s, including how they articulate their faith and personal commitment to change.

Hays, Edward M. *Pray All Ways: A Book for Daily Worship Using All Your Senses*. Easton, KS: Forest of Peace Books, 2007. Variety of prayers and prayer practices to enhance spirituality in daily life.

Horsley, Richard A. *Covenant Economics: A Biblical Vision of Justice for All*. Louisville: Westminster John Knox, 2009. Accessible exploration of economic issues in the Bible, including the call for action to people of faith.

Houston, Walter J. *Justice: The Biblical Challenge*. New York: Routledge, 2014. Scholarly study of the biblical concept of justice and how it can be applied to contemporary situations.

Jackson, Christal M., ed. *Women of Color Pray: Voices of Strength, Faith, Healing, Hope, and Courage*. Woodstock, VT: SkyLight Paths, 2005. Prayers, poetry, and meditations offered by women of color from across the globe.

Massaro, Thomas, SJ. *Living Justice: Catholic Social Teaching in Action*. Lanham, MD: Rowman & Littlefield, 2011. Accessible introduction to the principles of Catholic social teaching, including central themes, sources, and methods.

Myers, Ched, and Matthew Colwell. *Our God Is Undocumented: Biblical Faith and Immigrant Justice*. Maryknoll, NY: Orbis, 2012. Explores biblical themes of hospitality and welcoming strangers to the question of undocumented immigrants.

Pramuk, Christopher. *Hope Sings, So Beautiful: Graced Encounters Across the Color Line*. Collegeville, MN: Liturgical Press, 2013. Offers a "mosaic" of reflections to think and pray over the challenging issues of ethnic and racial encounter.

Sullivan, Susan Crawford, and Ron Pagnucco, eds. *A Vision of Justice: Engaging Catholic Social Teaching on the College Campus*. Collegeville, MN: Liturgical Press, 2014. Interdisciplinary resources compiled to facilitate understanding and action on issues of social justice.

GLORY TO THE FATHER
Glory to the Father,
   and to the Son,
   and to the Holy Spirit:
as it was in the beginning,
   is now,
   and will be for ever. Amen.

GLORIA AL PADRE
Gloria al Padre,
   y al Hijo,
   y al Espíritu Santo.
Como era en el principio,
   ahora y siempre,
   por los siglos de los siglos. Amén.

MORNING CANTICLE (Zechariah—*Benedictus*)
   Luke 1:68-79

Blessed be the Lord God of Israel,
   for he has looked favorably on his people and redeemed
      them.
He has raised up a mighty savior for us
   in the house of his servant David,
as he spoke through the mouth of his holy prophets from
     of old,
   that we would be saved from our enemies and from
     the hand of all who hate us.
Thus he has shown the mercy promised to our ancestors,
   and has remembered his holy covenant,
the oath that he swore to our ancestor Abraham,
   to grant us that we, being rescued from the hands of our
     enemies,
might serve him without fear, in holiness and righteousness
   before him all our days.
And you, child, will be called the prophet of the Most High;
   for you will go before the Lord to prepare his ways,
to give knowledge of salvation to his people
   by the forgiveness of their sins.
By the tender mercy of our God,
   the dawn from on high will break upon us,
to give light to those who sit in darkness and in the shadow of
    death,
   to guide our feet into the way of peace.

EVENING CANTICLE (Mary—*Magnificat*)
    Luke 1:47-55

My soul magnifies the Lord,
    and my spirit rejoices in God my Savior,
for he has looked with favor on the lowliness of his servant.
    Surely, from now on all generations will call me blessed;
for the Mighty One has done great things for me,
    and holy is his name.
His mercy is for those who fear him
    from generation to generation.
He has shown strength with his arm;
    he has scattered the proud in the thoughts of their hearts.
He has brought down the powerful from their thrones,
    and lifted up the lowly;
he has filled the hungry with good things,
    and sent the rich away empty.
He has helped his servant Israel,
    in remembrance of his mercy,
according to the promise he made to our ancestors,
    to Abraham and to his descendants forever.

NIGHT CANTICLE (Simeon—*Nunc Dimittis*)
    Luke 2:29-32

Master, now you are dismissing your servant in peace,
    according to your word;
for my eyes have seen your salvation,
    which you have prepared in the presence of all peoples,
a light for revelation to the Gentiles
    and for glory to your people Israel.

THE LORD'S PRAYER
Our Father, who art in heaven,
hallowed be thy name;
thy kingdom come,
thy will be done
on earth as it is in heaven.
Give us this day our daily bread,
and forgive us our trespasses,
as we forgive those who trespass against us;
and lead us not into temptation,
but deliver us from evil. Amen.

PADRE NUESTRO
Padre nuestro, que estás en el cielo,
santificado sea tu nombre;
venga a nosotros tu reino;
hágase tu voluntad en la tierra como en el cielo.
Danos hoy nuestro pan de cada día;
perdona nuestras ofensas,
como también nosotros perdonamos
a los que nos ofenden;
no nos dejes caer en la tentación, y líbranos del mal.
Amén.